MW01593743

ROCKY POINT

A True Life Story of Murder

By

Mark Siegel

THIRD MILLENNIUM PUBLISHING

A Cooperative of Online Writers and Resources

ISBN 1-929381-36-0
Viii, 243 pages

Michael McCollum
Proprietor
Third Millennium Publishing
1931 East Libra Drive
Suite 101
Tempe, AZ 85283
mccollum@3mpub.com

To Carole, my wife of 27 years, for putting up with this; to Bev Parker, for her hospitality, and to her late husband, Don Glasenapp, for his; and to Frenchy, T-Shirt, and the rest of the Rocky Pointers. To Kevin McAlonan, friend and editor, and Betty Brock Kantor for believing in this.

Table of Contents

The study of crime begins with the knowledge of oneself.
— Henry Miller

Go hence, to have more talk of these sad things;
Some shall be pardoned, and some punished;
For never was a story of more woe
Than this of Juliet and her Romeo.
— William Shakespeare

Prologue: Willoughby Arrested

If I were God, I'd be an agnostic. While capable of entertaining hypothetical versions of the truth, I lack absolute confidence in any reality, even my own. So my inclination is not to try to convince people that my version of events is sacred truth, but only that the official version may be wrong.

I am also a trial lawyer, and sometimes need to convince people that my version is sacred truth, but that's another story.

One night in 1995, a private investigator I call Grave Danger came to my house to deliver some information he'd obtained on a personal injury case I was trying. He could have phoned it in; actually he wanted to talk to me about a friend of his who was on death row. I told Grave I was a civil attorney not a criminal lawyer, but he said his friend was more interested in my credentials as a writer. The friend, Dan Willoughby, believed he had been unfairly convicted of murdering his wife and needed someone to help him get the "true story" out to the press.

Besides being pathologically skeptical, I am not a crusader.

I'd worked briefly as a muck-raking freelance journalist and also as a publisher of such books, but mostly what the experience had taught me was caution. I'd been approached by James Earl Ray's "agent" to see what kind of contract I'd be willing to offer on the story of his wrongful conviction for the assassination of Martin Luther King, Jr. I'd been asked to investigate the activities of an organized crime informant who was terrorizing citizens in Casa Grande, Arizona while under the protective wing of the witness protection program. A local publisher tried to interest me in doing a book on the continuing shenanigans of the Tyson family, two of whose murder convictions had wound up in front of the U.S. Supreme Court. I said no to projects like these because they were too dangerous. Solid citizens who do not know murderers romanticize what it means to become involved with them. I enjoy writing and talking, but I do not want to be sifting my children's teeth from the ashes of my burned house. When Grave Danger told me about the potential of being threatened by one of the investigators in Willoughby's case, I had the same reaction.

I took maybe five seconds to ponder the irony of being more afraid of the police than the supposed bad guys in this case. "I don't care which side of the law the threat comes from, Grave. If they threaten me because I'm stirring things up, I'm dropping the spoon back into the soup and going back to science fiction." I told him about pulling inflammatory chapters from a book I'd once written on the Internal Revenue Service on the basis of a single inquiring phone call from an IRS liaison officer.

But I'm also as curious as any cat whose luck has been holding steady at around four lives, and the Willoughby case looked like a fraud to me. Whether or not Willoughby truly was guilty, he had been railroaded by an extremely aggressive prosecution that defended its excesses with outrageous self-righteousness, a sort of piety a la mode I can't stand. As a skeptic, I don't write exposes that promise to reveal "the real truth." I do my best to reveal what is false, and Willoughby's conviction was shrouded with falsehoods.

On February 23, 1991, the Willoughby family was vacationing in Puerto Penasco, Mexico, a resort town on the Gulf of California known to Arizona tourists as Rocky

Point. My wife and I had camped on an estuary there fifteen years earlier, just before developers started building full-scale beach villas, like the one Dan and Trish Willoughby and their three kids rented. Late in the afternoon of the twenty-third, Dan's children, returning with him from an outing, discovered the comatose body of their mother in the bedroom of that rented beach house. Trish was lying face up on the bed. A towel was wrapped around her head and a knife was sticking out of her right temple. Her skull had been fractured in numerous places. Her body was practically floating on the blood-saturated mattress.

On December 11, 1991, the *Arizona Republic*, Phoenix's main newspaper at the time, announced:

Willoughby arrested

It's a banner headline over two large front-page photos. One of the photos shows a bespectacled, grey-haired man, in jail-house orange, handcuffed and flanked by two dark-suited detectives. Even in this photograph, Dan Willoughby appears miscast, an affable businessman who has no idea what he is doing in a Phoenix courtroom, dressed so inappropriately. He looks apologetic as he is crowded uncomfortably between the two burly cops. The second photo shows Sterling and Thera Huish, the parents of Dan's murdered wife, talking to reporters outside the courtroom. Sterling is looking to his sharp-faced wife for guidance. "All of the things I felt from the very beginning are now reality," Thera is quoted.

The things Thera apparently felt from the beginning included that Dan's marriage to Trish had been on the rocks; that Dan, having quit his own job months before, was financially dependent upon Trish, whose joint business with Thera was valued at approximately two and a half million dollars; that Dan had failed to break off his love affair with Yesenia Patino, even after it became public, and had no intention of abandoning the mysterious Mexican woman; and that Dan and Yesenia had conspired for months to murder Trish, and had consummated the plan in Rocky Point.

A companion article was entitled:

Transsexual also charged in murder.

Willoughby's arrest, ten months after the murder, occurred just four days after Yesenia Patino was arrested in Mazatlan, Mexico. Without her testimony, prosecutors knew they had no case against Dan, and Dan seems to have known it too. Yet no one was more shocked than Dan by the implications of the headline. Although he had made love countless times, Dan hadn't known his lover had had a sex-change operation until the police shocked him with the fact during his interrogation.

Arizona authorities had investigated Willoughby and pursued Yesenia Patino for many months following the murder. The evidence against Yesenia was irrefutable: her bloody fingerprints were found at the murder scene, including on knives stuck in the murdered woman's head. There was no hard evidence against Willoughby, but he was known to have been Yesenia's lover, and Thera Huish had accused him of murdering her daughter from the first moment she'd learned of the crime.

Legally there was some question Arizona authorities had any business working a murder that had occurred outside of the United States, yet Thera had little trouble convincing Kay Lines, an investigator from the Arizona Attorney General's Office, to involve several local law enforcement agencies in an immediate investigation of her son-in-law. Lines interrogated both Willoughby and Yesenia soon after the murder, but Yesenia disappeared from Phoenix the day before her crime scene fingerprints were confirmed, and he had no direct evidence against Willoughby. Throughout the spring and summer, investigators staked out Yesenia's apartment and interviewed friends and business acquaintances of the Willoughbys, but were unable to develop any specific proof. Then, during the summer of 1991, a lawsuit erupted between Dan Willoughby and Thera Huish over Trish's business insurance. Dan claimed that some of the proceeds from his wife's insurance belonged to him and his children, while Thera alleged publicly that Dan had murdered her daughter and wasn't entitled to a cent. Hard Copy aired a TV segment about the murder and the ensuing civil battle, including a photograph of Yesenia. That photograph resulted in Yesenia being recognized and apprehended in Mazatlan.

Following hours of interrogation, both on and off the recorder, Yesenia agreed to name Willoughby as a co-conspirator and co-murderer in exchange for immunity from prosecution in the United States. She said that Willoughby had planned the murder in Arizona and that Willoughby had insisted on striking the lethal blows himself, crushing his wife's skull with a homemade mace. Yesenia avowed that she only came in afterward and did the stabbing to make the scene look more like a robbery.

This story fit wonderfully with the Huish claim that Dan and Yesenia had murdered Trish Willoughby because she had made a small fortune by starting a mineral supplement distribution firm a few years before. Their marriage was on the rocks and Dan's extra-marital affair known to everyone in the family. Having lost his job as an air freight executive, Dan was reduced to working for his wife's company and reportedly despised his tenuous dependency. Trish's murder occurred on a vacation planned by Dan, in a beach house rented by Dan. Dan was the last person who had seen Trish alive — not counting Dan's transsexual lover.

All of these facts amount to a decent circumstantial case against Dan Willoughby — as long as you ignore the absence of any murder weapon, limited opportunity, the absence of any physical evidence that he was involved in the murder itself, and his complete lack of any violent criminal background or history of domestic violence.

Willoughby's first line of defense was jurisdictional. A December 11, 1991 headline read:

Mexican murder, U.S. plot: A tangle of 2 legal systems

Both countries wanted to prosecute the case, especially once suspects were in custody and success seemed likely, and each country technically could have filed extradition papers for the other's citizen. Mexico's claim, of course, was that the murder had been committed there and the Mexican government had an interest in showing tourists they were safe from random violence. The United States claimed that the atrocity had been committed against an American citizen and that the crime had been planned in the United States.

In the end, practical considerations prevailed. The Mexican government did not want to give Yesenia immunity when the murder evidence pointed so clearly to her and she had confessed to at least part of the crime. Without her testimony against Willoughby, they simply had no case against him. The United States, however, not only was willing to give her immunity, but, unlike Mexico, could seek the death penalty against either suspect.

David Ochoa, Willoughby's lawyer, argued and then appealed the jurisdictional issue, losing each time.

Bond for Willoughby denied

While it is not unusual for the Court to deny bail in a capital case, Willoughby soon suffered additional setbacks. Chief among them was Yesenia and other witnesses refusing to speak to defense attorney Ochoa, allegedly upon the instructions of the AG's Office. The AG's Office denied any wrongdoing.

Attorneys charge conspiracies in Willoughby case

Ochoa responded with new accusations concerning the irregularities in the autopsy conducted in Phoenix after Trish's body was exhumed. While the Mexican coroner had declared the cause of death to be the stab wounds, admittedly the work of Yesenia Patino, the Arizona coroner, examining the body in June of 1991, had found the cause of death to be the blunt-instrument blows to the skull, supposedly administered by Willoughby. Additionally, reports on the Arizona autopsy also revealed that Kay Lines, who had personally escorted the body from Mexico, had taken it on a side journey to another medical examiner prior to delivering it to the State's examiner — and that Lines had removed from the coffin a note written by Willoughby and placed in his wife's hands before burial. In it, Willoughby professed his innocence and promised to join his wife in heaven. When Ochoa moved to have the body exhumed a second time so that the note could be used at trial, his request was denied.

The AG's Office retaliated by alleging that Ochoa was attempting to persuade other witnesses to lie.

15 minutes are key in Rocky Point slaying

The Willoughby murder trial was a fiasco. The State contended that Willoughby and Yesenia had planned the murder in Arizona at length. They brought Yesenia's former husband and her brother to testify they had overheard snatches of such conversation. Ochoa did little cross-examination. The State brought Thera Huish to testify that her daughter had told her she was divorcing Dan, and that Dan was well aware that Trish was insured for nearly a million dollars. Ochoa did little cross-examination. The State examined Willoughby's adopted daughter, Marsha, who testified that, as Dan and the children were leaving for their excursion that fatal morning, Willoughby left them in their van for a few minutes while he went back into the beach house, supposedly to pick up his passport — but, according to the State, to bludgeon his wife to death. Ochoa did no cross-examination about the length of time Dan was in the house, the fact that he had no blood on his clothing when he emerged, or that Dan had invited Marsha back into the house with him and that she had declined. Finally, Yesenia Patino testified that Dan had planned the murder, had built a baseball sized steel mace on a piece of cord, and had used it to murder his wife while their children waited outside in the van. She said she only came into the house after Willoughby left to make the scene look like a robbery, while Trish was already dying, "making wheezing sounds like a chicken with its head cut off." Ochoa did not cross-examine her.

In fact, Ochoa did not call any witnesses at all in Dan's defense. He did not call the insurance agent who could have testified that Dan knew nothing of the million dollar life insurance policy — although it was that policy which allowed the State to seek the death penalty under a "murder for profit" statute. He did not call the

Willoughbys' babysitter and Trish's confidant to contradict Thera Huish's version of the Willoughbys' marriage. Most surprisingly, he did not confront Yesenia with a tape-recorded interview in which she explained that her testimony against Dan was false; that she was saying what the State wanted her to say in order to save herself.

When Willoughby frantically questioned his attorney as to what was going on, Ochoa told him point blank to shut up. "I'm the doctor. You're the patient. Let me operate." The operation apparently included Ochoa's unanticipated brainstorm in his opening statement that Willoughby and Yesenia "may have been involved in some kind of fraud together, but definitely they didn't intend to murder anybody." The judicial "surgery" concluded with Ochoa telling the jury in closing argument that the evidence didn't look good for his client. To no one's surprise, the patient died on the operating table.

Unbeknownst to his own client, Ochoa had spent the entire trial under the threat of felony charges for witness tampering — charges likely to be pursued or dropped at the request of the prosecuting attorneys he was sworn to oppose.

The headline in the *Arizona Republic* read:

Willoughby gets death in wife's killing
Still says he is innocent

On May 19, 1992, a jury convicted Dan Willoughby. The Arizona Supreme Court, which automatically reviews all death sentences, summed up the "facts" proven in this trial as follows:

Defendant and his wife, Trish, were residents of Phoenix, Arizona. In late 1990, Defendant arranged a trip to Puerto Penasco (Rocky Point), Mexico, ostensibly as a Christmas gift for Trish. The couple and their three children rented a condominium at Las Conchas beach for a weekend in February 1991. The day after the family arrived, Defendant and the children went to visit a nearby museum. Trish stayed behind because she was tired and wanted to rest.

After Defendant and the children boarded their van for the museum, Defendant returned to the condo, saying he forgot his passport. He remained in the condo for about five minutes. While he was inside, his oldest daughter tried to enter, but the door was locked. When Defendant came out of the condo, he was adjusting his belt and tucking in his shirt. After Defendant returned to the van, he and the children went on their trip.

When they returned some two hours later, Defendant's ten year old daughter Thera rushed in to tell her mother about the trip. She found her mother unconscious in the bedroom. Trish had been stabbed, bludgeoned, and strangled, and a knife was protruding from her head. Defendant gathered his children outside for prayer and then drove to the Red Cross station for help. Trish died that evening.

Mexican authorities questioned Defendant, who told them that he and his wife were happily married. They eventually released Defendant, and he arranged for the return of Trish's body to Arizona for burial. No autopsy was performed until Arizona authorities exhumed the body several months later.

After the murder, Defendant's mother-in-law told several people, including an investigator for the Attorney General's Office, that Defendant might have committed the murder. This prompted an investigation which revealed that, although he had appeared happily married, Defendant had been unhappy with his wife for the past several years.

Investigators discovered that in late 1990, Defendant met Yesenia Patino Gonzalez, a Mexican transsexual who was then "married" to Jack Mielke. After the purported marriage ceremony between Yesenia and Mielke, Mielke paid for Yesenia to have a male-to-female sex change operation. At all relevant times, Yesenia was a resident alien living in Arizona.

Defendant began an affair with Yesenia, took her on vacations, and paid the rent for her apartment. Trish eventually learned of the affair and confronted Yesenia. Defendant moved Yesenia to a different apartment. He also bought her an expensive engagement ring and told others, including Jack Mielke, that he wanted to marry Yesenia. He told Yesenia, however, that he could not divorce his wife because she "had too much on him."

Defendant, in fact, depended on Trish's income. She and her mother were sole partners in a business worth over $2.5 million, with a 1990 income of $324,000. Defendant, meanwhile, had lost his job, and he told Yesenia he would be "taken to the cleaners" if he tried to divorce Trish.

Defendant began to talk about killing his wife. Yesenia testified at trial that at various times Defendant discussed buying a firearm silencer in Mexico, drowning Trish while scuba diving, or pushing her off a cliff at the Grand Canyon. In May 1990, during a dinner with Yesenia and Jack Mielke at a Tempe restaurant, Defendant said "I think I will take her to Mexico and get rid of her." He later made similar statements to them at a restaurant in Cottonwood, Arizona. He also discussed having his "Mafia connections" kill her.

Defendant began discussing with Trish and her mother the disposition of their business should one of them die. He eventually convinced them to adopt an insurance-funded buy-out agreement. Several insurance policies covered Trish, including a $750,000 policy purchased just months before her murder.

Defendant began to plan the murder in more detail. He told Yesenia that he wanted the satisfaction of killing Trish. Yesenia was instructed to come in after the killing and make it look like a robbery by stabbing Trish, strangling her with a rope he bought, ransacking the condo, and taking her rings and money. Defendant rented a condo in Rocky Point, somewhat removed from others in the area, and paid in cash. Defendant and Yesenia made two trips from Phoenix to Rocky Point before the killing to reconnoiter the area and go over their plans. In Phoenix, Defendant showed Yesenia a weapon, described as a homemade mace consisting of a heavy ball attached by rope to a handle, he would use to kill Trish. He arranged for Yesenia's brother to take Yesenia to Rocky Point on the day of the murder.

On the afternoon of the killing, Defendant met Yesenia and her brother on the beach at Rocky Point. After Defendant and Yesenia talked, Defendant returned to the condo. Yesenia left her brother at a park and drove to a spot with a view of the condo. After Defendant and the children left for the museum, she went to the condo and entered through an unlocked back door. Taking knives from the kitchen, Yesenia went to the bedroom and saw Trish lying comatose in a pool of blood. Trish was still breathing, each breath making a gurgling sound. Following Defendant's plan, Yesenia stabbed and strangled Trish but was unable to kill her. After taking Trish's rings and money and scattering the contents of Trish's purse, Yesenia fled, meeting her brother for the return trip to Arizona.

At the border, a United States Customs agent understood Yesenia to say that she and her brother were going to a store just across the border. When the agent saw that they did not go there, she had them returned to the port of entry and searched. Trish's rings were discovered in Yesenia's pocket, but because no contraband was discovered, Yesenia and her brother were released. They immediately returned to Phoenix.

After the murder, Defendant took steps to cover his tracks. He told Yesenia to leave Phoenix, and she returned to Mexico. Defendant called a meeting of his neighbors, at which he denied involvement in the killing and tried to dissuade them from talking to police. He asked Yesenia's brother to lie to police about seeing Defendant in Mexico. He threatened Jack Mielke and told him not to get involved. He called his travel agent to have the trip information removed from the agent's computer. He asked his former secretary to tell police he was a wonderful family man and told her to threaten a co-worker to prevent him from telling police about Defendant and Yesenia. He lied to investigators, saying that guards at the condo had seen three Indians in a black pick-up truck in the area. He collected on an older life insurance policy for his wife but was unsuccessful in collecting on the policy purchased to fund the buyout agreement between Trish and her mother.

A Maricopa County grand jury indicted Defendant for premeditated first-degree murder and conspiracy to commit one or more of the following offenses: murder, fraudulent schemes and artifices, armed robbery, obstructing a criminal investigation or prosecution, and filing a fraudulent insurance claim. Yesenia was charged with murder by the Mexican authorities, pleaded guilty, and was sentenced to life in prison. During the investigation, the Mexican government cooperated with Arizona officials by allowing them to interview Yesenia and giving them temporary custody of her so that she could testify at the three-week trial. In return for turning state's evidence, the state agreed not to prosecute Yesenia and to try to have her sentence in Mexico reduced.

The defense called no witnesses and rested immediately after the state's case concluded. The jury *convicted Defendant of both the murder and conspiracy counts. After the aggravation/mitigation hearing, the trial judge found one aggravating circumstance--that the murder was committed in expectation of pecuniary gain-- and no mitigating circumstances. He sentenced Defendant to death for the murder and life imprisonment for the conspiracy conviction.*

With this satisfying, apparently irrefutable certainty, the cell door slammed and the public quickly forgot about the murder. Thera Huish not only got all of her daughter's business, she took nearly all the life insurance as well, although the Willoughbys' children should have been beneficiaries. David Ochoa, previously reprimanded by the Arizona Supreme Court for incompetence, took a hiatus from the practice of criminal law, leaving Dan penniless to conduct an appeal. The successful state prosecutor was a big hit on the local talk show circuit and went into private practice for himself.

From death row, Dan Willoughby contacted me.

This is what I learned.

Chapter 1: Sunset Ceremony

People who've read no more than newspaper accounts of the Willoughby murder are unanimous in their condemnation of Dan Willoughby. This is partly because his side of the story was never properly told, but it also has to do with the bizarre facts of the murder, the alien character of the players. It is far easier to believe that someone who behaves in a weird way, looks extreme, and has a history of unusual acts would commit a heinous murder. Think of the almost universally stunned responses of television interviewees as they report that the neighbor boy who just sprayed his grammar school with the guts of his playmates seemed like a normal kid, a quiet boy with nice parents. Who would have suspected? In Willoughby's case, we ask, what kind of man takes a transsexual lover with psychotic tendencies into the bosom of his peaceful, middle-class family? Certainly not someone like you or me. . . .

Between the act and the understanding comes the tourist. We are here after the fact — after the volcanic eruption, the tidal wave, the Diaspora or historic stagecoach robbery — our minds clad in Hawaiian prints, gawking through viewfinders.

Until I decided to look into the Willoughby murder, I hadn't been down to Puerto Peñasco, the Sonoran town gringos call Rocky Point, since the early Seventies, when Carole and I had gotten the old VW stuck in the sand dunes she *insisted* were a road. The two of us nearly came to blows over it before a crew of Mexican construction workers toting a plastic garbage bag full of beer and ice happened by and dug us out. As it happens, our ancient camping spot, east of town on a bare and beautiful estuary, was quite near where the murder occurred. It's impossible to pinpoint our old spot because of the soul-obliterating development that has occurred in the interim. My vision of the beach house in which Trish Willoughby was bludgeoned and stabbed overlays my image of our distant summer's idyll in freakish double-exposure.

Although we've come to look at the scene of the Willoughby murder, we're staying with acquaintances on the other side of Puerto Peñasco, and so head west off the highway down a dirt road. Clearly this is the way to the gringos' encampment. It is distinguished from other unsigned dirt roads by the presence of twenty or so curio stands selling t-shirts and fireworks to tourists. Everybody calls this stretch Rodeo Drive. "You know," a Mexican man in a stained brown shirt grins through a very few teeth, "like in Beverly Hells." This town's greatest resource is its sense of irony.

When we hit Cholla Bay, about three miles further along the rutted sandpack, there are still no street signs, and, where numbers are visible on the houses, they don't run consecutively. Carole's directions, taken down during a telephone conversation only the night before, seem completely foreign to her, as if they're a treasure map in foreign hand she's discovered in the attic. The one clear landmark in her notes, "Chi Chi's," is just not findable. It might be any one of a dozen boarded-up or burned-out shops we pass, its hulk still vividly reminiscent of Chi Chi's to the locals, but invisible in our own gringo dimension. The dead, images frozen, often are remembered more distinctly than the living.

The dunes on the western end of town limit vision to fifty yards in any direction and are no help in finding the beach house. Neither is the smell of the salt sea breeze, because the ocean saturates the air, its presence everywhere at once. But still it is difficult to get profoundly, LA-style lost. We drive around, away from the cardboard and pressed tin shacks where the locals live, heading always down-dune, because, I suppose, subconsciously the thought of the ocean being uphill, restrained only by shifting piles of sand, is incomprehensibly frightening. Finally a local boy points toward a section of town described as "muy richo." We protest guiltily, "Non," but we mean "not in our world."

Then we crest the last high dune above the bay and overlook the Gulf of California — or the Sea of Cortez, as non-Californians prefer to call it. Most of the local "mansions" were built by foreigners over the past twenty years for the cost of putting up a new garage in the US, and garages are what some resemble. The gringo homes on the bay are round or square or both. Many began as trailers but then sprouted wooden appendages. Some have roofs tilted toward the sun, others are flat, but all share a single genetic anomaly: one, two, or three water tanks, five-foot-high ceramic jugs, like giant nipples on every roof. These ocean-front dwellings resemble a colony of strange aquata, beached among the granite cliffs and volcanic rock and indifferent to the brown-skinned folks who crabwalk among them or rip along the hard-packed veins of sand on ATVs or tiny motor scooters.

It is hot and humid in the late afternoon sun, and the dust blows even harder along the shoreline. An hour before sundown we finally find the vacation home of Bev and Don. "That can't be it," I observe, pondering the details of Carole's treasure map. "Where's the orange trim? Or the arches?"

"That's it," she shrugs.

"Maybe Don got it confused with a McDonald's," I suggest. "But he's an engineer. Engineers don't get confused. They confuse others."

"My point exactly. But this is it," she assures me.

"But he said it's the only two story structure in the neighborhood. He was very specific. Unless all these other places shot up overnight —"

"This is it," she says again. "Bev is waving to us from the veranda."

"Well, that is the Del Mar Motel over there," I concede, downshifting into second for the crawl up the last sand dune. "I guess this could be it."

You *can* see the house when looking up from the beach, as Carole's treasure map predicted — it and at least thirty of the forty other homes in this enclave. It is not on the beach, as I have imagined, but several hundred thoroughly inhabited yards back and fifty rocky yards up from the water.

It is a real house, though, with plenty of rooms and a corrugated cathedral of a work-and-storage garage which Don, a retired engineer, is pleased to show me about three minutes after we arrive. The kitchen is open to a living room furnished in that sturdy, autumnal upholstery that absorbs wet sand and soda with minimal damage. The living room in turn opens onto the veranda, overlooking the bay to the west.

Bev is Carole's friend, a long-time acquaintance from the hospital where both had worked, first as nurses and then, as the possibility of contracting a nightmare plague from a patient became uncomfortably real, in the bloodless world of utilization review and auditing. Bev is graying, tanned, and, I know from previous encounters, a killer conversationalist. Don, who took early retirement from one of the Blue Chips, is her second husband, or her third, and I have only met him before to shake hands. He too is tan, and in his mid-fifties still looks good without a shirt, which maybe he has left off for my benefit rather than Carole's.

He offers a really firm handshake, a standard pawn to king four opening among guys.

"Nice house," I respond.

"Wait 'til you see the workshop," he advises.

I hold my play, having heard unpleasant things about him from a carpenter friend of mine with whom he'd had a fist fight a few years ago. Bev, too, has complained to Carole about Don's volatile temper and numerous other failings, but then I am fairly certain he has heard similar things about me from my own, at times, outrageously unfair wife. So like I say, my own introduction is a traditional, reserved, and noncommittal shuffling of pieces — knowing that, soon enough, fueled by alcohol and cheese whiz, my horses suddenly will jump over the line of pawns and I'll be off on some mad, bizarre attack. I wonder if I've always been this way, or if worrying about getting old is making me old.

Six or seven people were in the living room and on the veranda when we arrived, and another six drift in while we park our bags and stash the car behind the garage. A few are young beach campers Bev met earlier that day and invited up to use her shower. They've mingled instantly with the "regulars," neighbors who abandoned their lives in various other places to live in Cholla Bay, yet apparently find their own homes less interesting than someone else's, even here in Mexico. They are like ghosts twice removed, welcoming the strangers warmly if cryptically, while waiting for the sun to set. We fit right in.

I am drawn to a specter named Frenchy, an Italian born in Pennsylvania and raised in Algiers. He served in someone's navy in World War II and then stayed away from Africa when the Arabs kicked out the Europeans in the late Forties. For many years, he and his wife operated a small Italian restaurant outside of Erie, PA. His wife died of cancer last year and he is still in shock, a state of deceptively cheerful loneliness that reveals itself in endless reminiscing. This is fine with me, since I am sick to death of my own stories. Like me, he drinks whatever he is offered and smiles thoughtfully at whatever is said. I bet he, too, gets most of his drinking glasses two at a time, whenever there is a close-out sale on gift boxes of scotch.

In the meantime, Carole is taking a profound and instant dislike to a drunken helicopter pilot named Rex. Thin but broad-shouldered, with a narrow brown mustache, Rex has strong opinions about everything. Many probably occur to him for the first time even as he speaks, although they seem to have belonged to him always, unexamined inheritances trunked up in a brain-attic, trotted out in complete disregard of the enlightened sensibilities of this more modern age.

"You're a lawyer," Rex tells me, then launches into a story about a flying gig in the Amazon. "The laws are more practical down there. In Brazil I had this job flying prostitutes around in the jungle."

Something of a feminist, Carole politely squirts gin and tonic out of her nose and stares at me as if I am the one saying this.

"It was a law, see? You have to have one prostitute for every jungle work crew of ten men. Thing is, they don't send along a pimp or anything, so somehow I end up having to protect their interests, sort things out with their customers. And of course, everyone assumes I should be getting it on the side from all the girls. It's an international convention —"

I figure he has not long to live. Carole's remarkable calms can be, and usually are, deceptive. I excuse myself momentarily from Frenchy when I see her move to the kitchen counter, and the cutlery. She begins slicing up limes for gin and tonics and for the beers with a little paring knife, way more limes than we'll need if we drink until dawn. She is angry at me for not doing something about Rex. This pisses me off.

Out on the veranda, where I go in search of fellow misunderstood husbands, I suddenly feel the actual violence in my own disposition. Never to be realized, of course. Of course. A salt breeze is blowing off the bay while the humidity, so novel to us Arizonans, sticks my shirt to my back, making my most immediately important task to pluck it free without spilling my drink.

A woman was brutally murdered here?

Life is a comedy of manners in which, despite having played our roles adequately in previous seasons, we are currently miscast. My announced purpose in coming to Mexico, to write an investigative page-turner about the bizarre and spectacular Willoughby murder, is mostly an excuse to feel as good as I can feel about the ocean, the beach, and a free bed. I am searching for something like Ozzie Nelson's job, whatever it was, a job that served to let him bumble amiably through another episode with Harriet and the kids. Up until now, the Willoughby murder itself has seemed no more real to me than the possibility that my wife, who, as far as I know, has never tried to hurt anyone physically, will puncture the local sexist bore with her tiny lime knife as she politely hands him a gin and tonic. But then a single drop of rain falls from the clear sky. The sensation of the water on my skin reminds me of Dan Willoughby, the real man, the way none of the rest of this trip has.

Dan has been losing his tan in the Florence penitentiary, and only recently experienced weather for the first time since his arrest in 1991. J. Fife Symington had been elected governor of Arizona on the premise that the state needed a businessman to instill Fiscal Responsibility into a state government that already was close to dead last in funding education and social services. He was re-elected in the midst of declaring bankruptcy and being investigated, sued, and indicted for financial shenanigans by the RTC. With irony circling his gubernatorial career like a vulture, Symington decided to divert attention from his business and legal fiascos with a new platform: being Tough On Crime.

To show the citizens of Arizona he is Tough On Crime as well as Fiscally Responsible, Fife ordered Death Row inmates to work on chain gangs rather than fritter away the taxpayers' money sitting in cells waiting to die. Accordingly, a dozen inmates had been shackled together by hand- and leg-irons and transported under heavy guard to an arid desert plot a mile from the prison. This must have caused a moment of consternation to the prisoners, who had heard reports of public impatience with enforcement of the State's death penalty. Also, Arizona's penal system had been condemned repeatedly by the federal courts for its abuses, so the announcement that they were to "clean up" this arid stretch of desert might well have been a cruel joke. Their hands were unshackled, but not their legs, and there was no way they could be given gardening tools, any of which might serve as weapons. The Dirty Dozen hand-weeded the desert for eight hours without a break, under the scrutiny of eight guards itching to deploy some nonlethal buckshot, while the bus driver slept in the shade of his bus, and motorists on car phones called in the sighting ("Dead Men Gardening") to a local radio station which delights in tracking such events. Economically, it doesn't make a lot of sense to me, but then I wasn't elected governor based on my financial acumen.

From the prisoners' points of view, it was even harder to figure out. When the shackled cons were first herded out of the bus into the desert lot and lined up in front of the heavily armed guards, they were waiting to dig their own graves. But then something very un-Arizona happened. A light rain began to fall.

It was the first rain Dan had felt in two and a half years. When he realized he was standing with his face raised and his eyes and mouth wide open, he looked around in embarrassment only to find many of the other death-rowers, hardened inmates convicted of heinous homicidal acts, doing exactly the same thing.

It was an amazing day, Dan said. The sound of traffic on the freeway, the flinty scent of the desert air after a rain, the sky, the wind — the horizon, for God's sake. *No bars.* I can't imagine what it meant to him. When the wind died down, he thought he could hear children playing.

After this first day of Symington's new Get Tough plan, inmates deluged the guards with queries about the next work detail. They were told Symington was rethinking the experiment.

Which brings me back to the bugs in my own plan. I have more bugs than plan, which is not always a bad thing, actually; if you have enough bugs to work out, you never have to deal with the plan itself. That has been my modus operandi of late, Ozzie-Nelson-proofing my life. That is how I've gotten through the last year, while Dan thoughtlessly wasted my tax dollars on death row and wrote letter after letter asking me about the book he hopes will help free him. But now, here I am, undertaking some action, however trivial, and hunkering down with my martini behind the diversion provided by Rex's sexism.

Not that the book will free Dan. Or me. The more I have investigated the crime, the more I am sure of that. But I would like to get the particulars right, to come to an understanding. If Dan Willoughby committed a crime, I imagine it began something like this: he's drinking with friends, in an airport bar maybe, makes an offhand joke in front of his mistress about killing his wife and running off to Mexico with her money to lose themselves in lust. Yesenia's a Mexican national who has run off to the United States for a good time, so they already are not on the same page, but this makes my scenario all the more likely. A mistress needs constantly to be impressed. So Dan says it, hoping for a laugh and a blow job, and a while later Yesenia and her brother Tony are in their pickup, on the way to surprise the sleeping wife.

It is this kind of normal impulse, to impress a woman, to lunge for some too-good-to-pass-up freebie, it is this sort of impulse, suddenly thrown off the tracks of life's roller coaster to career out of control at a surprise curve, of which Rex best be aware.

I am choosing a skinny blonde girl from among the beach people to be my imaginary mistress (she is clad, as far as I can tell, only in an over-sized black t-shirt and earrings that look like fish hooks), when Rex himself, as will be his habit over the next few days, interrupts my thoughts. "Sun'll be going down in exactly seven minutes," he says, and, ignoring the martini halfway to my mouth, hands me a Tecate. "You better take this."

Don appears at Rex's elbow, circles him, and places himself between the two of us, much like a hockey player rushing back on defense. Rex is trying to recruit all the men, even me, for a fishing trip that will never happen tomorrow, because, as everyone but Rex will admit, the ocean is too rough. "*Mañana, maybe* is the motto of this place," Don jokes when Rex continues to insist on my participation, and a second later they are re-embroiled in a debate about tomorrow's weather. Rex insists that, while there will be cloud cover, the swells will be no more than two or three feet if we get out by six a.m. Rex states this with the precision of a timetraveler who has been there and back and has taken careful measurements with the best scientific equipment. He is predicting the number and quality of the fish he will catch, when the other guests, led by Bev, begin to file out onto the veranda.

The nightly Sundown Ceremony is set to commence. Cameras click tentatively. Carole circles the back of the crowd, then approaches and reproaches me about my aloofness. I explain that Rex wanted to talk about important guy things.

Don quiets us all and makes a brief, half-solemn speech about drinking with friends at day's end. The sun becomes enormous as it touches the ocean, engorged on seawater as it turns from yellow to orange and red.

"Just before it goes under, it gives off this green flash," Rex informs us.

Her camera halfway to her face, Carole pauses to inform this village idiot that this green flash is only an optical illusion, or perhaps a digestion problem.

"If you hit your shutter at just the right moment," he says undaunted, "you can get it on film."

"On cheap film," Carole mutters.

"I'll tell you when," Rex promises authoritatively.

Carole gives me a murderous look predicting that, when confronted with a picture showing no green, Rex will claim that she snapped the shutter at the wrong moment. I stare at the sunset through both my beer and my martini, but don't really perceive a green. Rum might work better. This martini sunset looks blood red, more the color you'd expect in Beverly Hells.

I turn to Frenchy, who has joined us, but he merely shrugs and smiles. I smile back, and we toast the sun and sea snuffing out this day in 1995. We toast the sunset at length. And condemned murderers. And dead dreams.

I wish Rex were right, that if we clicked the shutter of our mental cameras at just the right moment we would be sure to catch some ineffable truth among the broad, shifting spectrum of events. But I am more of Carole's school of thought. We do our best to take a clear picture so that we can examine the moment more carefully, only to have some fool second-guess us, tell us we took the wrong picture at the wrong time – and, most aggravatingly, to know he might be right.

Between the act and the understanding comes the tourist. We are here after the fact, minds clad in Hawaiian prints, gawking through viewfinders. Later, using our feelings as an index, we will sort out the blurred and severed images. Or perhaps we will leave it all in the back of a drawer, undeveloped, unexamined, eventually to be forgotten.

Those of us at this party have that choice. We will talk about Dan in prison and Trish in her grave, and the other players in this drama, and perhaps we even will take something back to our own marriages, and to our affairs — for, at bottom, this apparently freakish horror show makes perfect sense in the context of our own very average lives.

Chapter 2: Feb. 22, 1991: The Keystone Getaway

At trial, the prosecution claimed Tony Patino, Yesenia's brother, was no more than an uninvolved witness to the events of February 22, 1991. He was with Yesenia both immediately before and after the murder, yet had no specific knowledge of it. On cross examination, Willoughby's lawyer, David Ochoa, failed to bring out the fact that Tony had been arrested as an accomplice and the charges against him had been dropped in exchange for cooperating with the prosecution. In fact, Ochoa chose to announce to the jury that Tony himself had nothing to do with the murder, a real jaw-dropper considering there was more evidence linking Tony to the scene than Dan himself.

Although Tony was an illegal alien at the time of his arrest and testimony, he continues to live in the United States.

Tony's luck seems to be in what he remembers and what he doesn't. According to Tony, his sister asked him to drive her to Rocky Point the night before the murder. She told him they were going there so she could pick up some money that was owed Dan. Dan always was lending people money — to neighbors who couldn't make mortgage payments and to people like Tony, when he needed a down payment for his pickup truck. His sister was always embroiling Tony in extreme schemes, and he didn't want to go, but when she said it was pay-back time for Dan he couldn't very well refuse the use of his truck.

Based on his and Yesenia's testimony and on the sparse physical evidence, this is how I first imagined the second half of that afternoon:

Tony watched the silver pick-up truck jerking up the street to his left. She was ruining the fucking engine, not to mention the clutch. As he saw her come around the corner, Tony tossed the roach he'd been worrying into the gutter. He moved into the driver's seat as soon as she clunked to a halt in front of him, then gunned the engine, making sure the motor was actually running, before he even looked at her.

"Jesus, you wore that?" he asked as she resettled herself onto the seat next to him. He thought she'd had a little black hat, like the French wore, in her bag, but now she had a ski mask on.

Yesenia laughed breathlessly and plucked the black ski mask from her head.

"Did you get the money?"

"The money? Yeah, I got what I came for."

"You got shit all over your sleeve, Sis," Tony said. She smelled weird, like the big dog in their old house in Chihuahua after it humped the bitch next door.

"No problem," she said, rolling the white polka-dot blouse up to the elbow of the right arm. "Don' worry, nothing will get on the seat. I've thought of everything."

Tony grimaced. He was no genius himself, but at least he knew it. His sister was crazy, but thought she was inspired.

There was sand all over the floor of the truck, hardly a novelty in Rocky Point, but he guessed the place she'd come from. Dozen of beach houses, lined two deep up from the edge of the bay, were already completed. Some of the spaces between these houses were under construction now, and a third row of buildings were nearly done. Despite the Mexican government's supposed opposition, the Los

Conchas development was selling beach bungalows to gringos as fast as it could build them. Through their bank trusts, the gringos, mostly from Arizona, owned nearly every one of the new homes, while the natives of Puerto Penasco, Sonora, dwelt in their cardboard and tin shacks on the other side of the security gate through which Yesenia must have passed. "You drove through the security gate wearing that ski mask?"

"I just put it back on for you, bro."

All of it was just another game for Yesenia. She'd driven him in and out of the development earlier in the day to test the security. She'd told the guard they had to drop off some construction tools. This was fine with the gatekeeper, who was really only worried about people taking construction equipment and supplies out of the development. He probably hadn't even been curious about the dark-skinned woman driving out in an empty truck this time and just waved her through. "You didn't flirt with the guard, did you? You always make everyone suspicious."

"I just wanted to see if he was using his phone."

"He doesn't have no damn phone."

"I know. It was like I owned the place," *laughed Yesenia.* "Maybe I'll buy it," *she said as a happy after-thought,* "if they put in a phone." *She thought she'd be rich soon.*

Tony wanted to hit her in the face, but he didn't dare. The things she did were crazy. He knew his sister was capable of anything.

They followed the beaten sand road between the dunes until it turned into pavement. To the right, the sign said, was the Cedo. Tony didn't know exactly what that was, though Yesenia talked about it as if she had a membership to the place. He was pretty sure she didn't know what it was either. He turned left.

It was a couple miles back into Puerto Penasco. Tony could tell Yesenia wanted to stop at Arturo's to celebrate, but she had promised him solemnly they would get out of town right after it happened. The gay bar gave him the creeps, anyway. It didn't make him feel like a rooster in a hen house. More like a hen trying to keep an eye on the farmer. You think he would have been used to it after all these years.

When they hit Route 8 he turned right onto the pavement, heading north. Seeing the Tecate franchise and then the Corona made him thirsty; they beckoned to him like whores on pay day. It made him feel a little sick, a little queasy, but he didn't let himself think about it. If they stopped along the curb, the little kids would run up with their squeegees and try to extort money for spreading their spit around on his windshield. After spending time in the United States, Tony observed almost reflexively that a lot of these crumbling walls needed paint. On the other hand, there were only a few broken, roofless, and empty buildings. This was a relatively prosperous section of Puerto Penasco, a main commercial district. They passed the baseball stadium that all the tourists thought was for bull fights. Then he passed the turn-off for Cholla Bay, the last real street left before leaving town, and he felt himself being drawn north, like a big magnet was pulling his chest toward safety. That was when he saw the red flags up ahead.

"Relax," Yesenia said. "It's just those damn kids and their ambulancia."

She was right. Two Mexican boys had placed orange cones along the center of the road and were waving down tourist traffic heading both ways down the major highway, looking for donations to keep the ambulance service running. The big white van with its red crosses stood directly opposite them on the side of the road.

"We should stop and make a donation," Yesenia laughed. "After all, we'll be using their services."

"I don't have any money."

"I've got some now," Yesenia reminded him. "It was supposed to look like a robbery." But he drove right by them. Yesenia craned around in her seat again, watching them recede. "You didn't stop!"

"You got blood all over you."

"No I don't. You can't see nothing."

"Well, they could probably smell it. They work with that stuff all day long."

It was a little over a hundred kilometers, sixty miles, to the border. Somewhere along the way, Tony wasn't exactly sure where, Yesenia suddenly opened her window and tossed the bundle out.

"What the hell are you doing?" he asked.

"We had to get rid of it somewhere. This was as good a place as any."

"We could 'a taken it back into the desert and buried it."

"Tony," she laughed as if he were an imbecile, "that would have been suspicious."

She was right about that. There was so much crap littering the highway, paper, bottles, cans, pieces of clothing and other garbage, that Yesenia's trash would hardly be noticed.

Tony navigated the pick-up through the curves on the outskirts of Sonoyta. The speed limits became ridiculous, but Tony obeyed them scrupulously, knowing they might be enforced in the border town. He stopped at a junction. One way headed toward the Border Internacianala, the other toward Caborca. Tony had a vague, uncomfortable recollection there was a state prison in Caborca.

"Get out of the truck," Yesenia said suddenly.

"What are you talking about?"

"I'm gonna drive."

"Like hell you are. You already ruined my clutch. We'll just drive right through. Say what we always say."

"You don't have citizenship, Tony. You don't even have a Green Card. I don't want 'em stoppin' us because you don't have your Green Card."

"I speak good English," he protested vainly.

"Look, just get out and walk through, like you're doin' a little shoppin'. I'll pick you up on the other side."

It was crazy, but Tony said OK just to get away from her for a while. If she was going to insist on fucking up and getting herself busted at the border, he at least would be able to make a run for it. "OK. Give me some money. So I can show them, about the shopping." When she did, he inspected the bills for bloodstains.

As he was showing the border guard the American dollars, he saw out of the corner of his eye Yesenia roll up to the stop sign in front of the nearest check point. He was afraid to look because she might wave or wink or something, like it was all a big game everybody was in on.

He walked a block up the street and waited where he knew she would have to turn to head up toward Phoenix. What was taking her so long? He knew she was concocting another one of her incredible stories. Why the hell couldn't she just say she was going shopping, like everybody else sneaking across the border? His name was on the registration of the goddamn pickup.

When she finally pulled up to where he waited, he started cursing at her even before he got into the truck.

"No problem," she said. "I told them I was on my way to my wedding. I told them I was going up to Arizona to marry a rich man. A millionaire."

"You gonna invite the police to the wedding?" Tony sneered. Then as she smiled he cursed again. "You didn't, did you?!"

As they pulled away from the curb, Tony looked behind them. He thought he saw the border guard looking at the truck.

Yesenia's laugh was high-pitched and loud, really distinctive. Like everything else about his sister, it called attention to her no matter where she was. Tony hated it. Right now it was the last thing in the world he wanted to hear.

"We've done it!" she said.

Tony couldn't see a reason not to believe her. But about ten miles further north, as they were passing through something called the Organ Pipe National Monument, he spotted the United States Border Patrol car following them. He knew the station was just up ahead, and hoped the car was going there. Then its lights came on and signaled them to pull over. "What have you got on you?" he asked his sister as she slowed the vehicle to a stop.

"Nothing," she said.

"I don't believe you," he said. "What have you got?"

"Just the rings. I told the border guard they were my wedding rings. They're just a little small, that's all. I told him I was gonna lose a little weight."

Tony looked at his sister's bony frame, a little too muscular for a normal woman, and shook his head in disgust.

I've seen the road, read the police interviews with Tony Patino. Tony admitted to investigators that he drove his sister Yesenia to Rocky Point on the day of the murder in his silver Ford pickup, and that Yesenia went off to the beach house where Trish Willoughby was killed while he waited elsewhere. Tire tracks were found in this location by Mexican police... .

But when do you know enough to know what you know?

Siegel

Chapter 3: Museums

When they were stopped on the day of the murder, the Border Patrol ordered Tony and Yesenia Patino to follow them back to Immigration for questioning. As usual, Tony said little and Yesenia said too much. But, while Yesenia's behavior at the border crossing would have been suspicious in a movie, her very incompetence prevented real-life police from taking her seriously at first. They asked Yesenia about a handful of rings they found in her purse — the rings which, in fact, she had stolen from the woman she'd just murdered. Yesenia said they were her engagement and wedding rings from her wealthy American husband. The border cops asked why the rings didn't fit her then, and she explained she'd meant she was about to be married and the rings, from her future wealthy American husband's mother, had yet to be sized for her.

The bemused officials did not detain the pair. There were no reports of stolen rings on the American side of the border, and Trish Willoughby's body had not even been discovered yet. The Border Patrol's sole interest was Tony's citizenship: he'd been spotted getting back into the pick-up truck.

All witnesses agree that, while the Patinos were making their Laurel-and-Hardyesque escape, Dan Willoughby was with his children at an oceanside museum called the Cedo, and then checking out the carcass of a whale that had beached nearby.

My first visit, after a quick lunch back at Bev's, is to this museum, to measure its proximity to the scene of the crime and to discuss the whale with locals to see what sort of distraction it might have provided. Don has agreed to drive us, while Bev decides to stay home to nap (seeing the irony but, being a practical person, ignoring it).

After the blandness of your neighbors' Suburbans and BMWs and Camrys, Mexican vehicles are real eye-candy. The law in Rocky Point seems to be that, if it doesn't have a windshield or doors, it's not a car, and so you don't have to pay to register it and don't have to have a license to drive it. Sensible locals, therefore, construct their vehicles out of old farm equipment, ATVs, boats, and the like. There are a lot of wooden parts. People often sit on top instead of inside. My favorite, a motorized fishing boat on an extended ATV frame, circles Bev's house at night with a single bulb glowing on top of a ten foot antenna, looking like a bioluminescent monster from the deep. Bedrock has nothing on Rocky Point for this kind of glam.

Don drives, while imparting the two things he knows about the Cedo: not unlike the local motor vehicles, it is made completely out of tires and aluminum cans; and it is no more than half a mile from the Willoughby bungalow as the crow flies, when it flies across sand dunes, and three or four miles by road, when the road goes around the dunes. I'm surprised by the proximity, which hardly seems to make for an airtight alibi.

Museums are supposed to offer certainty, moments of official history frozen in time. But just like everything else related to this adventure, the Mexican museum provides pretty much the opposite experience.

The Cedo turns out to be quite small, as is its gift shop, to which we gringos soon gravitate. There are more places to spend money per block in Rocky Point than in the U.S., but fewer official places. Official places to spend money are gringo magnets. However, this gift shop has few things for sale, and we have purchased all of them in a matter of minutes. The shop is dedicated not to commerce but to the ecology of Rocky Point. One wall of the gift shop is itself a cut-away exhibit, displaying the construction of old tires and aluminum cans covered with a concrete mix derived solely from local sands and plants. Also on display is the primitive string-and-stake tool used in laying out the structure; perhaps part of the local "ecology" is its architectural resources, the resourcefulness of its people, the very mind-set that allows one to live among detritus and make a world of it. Yesterday's newspaper is tomorrow's piñata.

This ability to rebuild out of what the ocean leaves you is something else I have lost. Revealing one's superstructure to create an illusory bond between observer and builder, on the other hand, is a strategy with which I am familiar, in literature and life.

The kids showed respectful interest when Dan explained the museum to them, but were obviously far most intrigued by the skeleton of the fifty-five-foot fin whale mounted along the roadside next to the building. The skull alone was bigger than the family's Bronco and looked like a space craft. The ribs stood twelve feet high. But it only prepared them for the real spectacle when the curator of the Cedo, during his hour-long tour of the library and research facility, casually announced another whale had beached itself recently just a few hundred yards from the museum. Seven-year-old Hayden and eleven year old Thera weren't sure they'd heard right and looked to their leader, Marsha, for confirmation. The fifteen-year-old had only been their sister since the previous year when she had been dumped by another foster family, but Marsha had retained a certain suspicion of adults despite her own outward maturity. She was of the world of children, and knew instinctively that death is best studied in the flesh.

As soon as the curator released them, they raced down to the beach to ogle the huge carcass. Did they sense the thing was not just another dead fish, but an amazing machine now abandoned by an intelligence the size of a Volkswagen? What did Dan, watching from the shade of the museum's wall, feel when confronted with the fact that a creature so powerful and sentient might be unable to perform the simple task of turning itself away from obvious self-destruction?

The whale was so big that local volunteers had been unable to drag it out of the shoals in time to save its life. When it died, they tied it up to an assortment of ATVs, dune buggies, and doorless pick-up trucks and just managed to drag it a little further up onto the beach, past the tide line, where this carnival procession left it to be buried.

Today's spectacle would stink in tomorrow's sun. After the microbes did their work behind earthen curtains, reducing the mammoth's awful weight, the carcass would be hauled away. Or perhaps the skeleton would become another display, reconstructed for the benefit of the curious, the bones fleshed out again by their imagination. The children ran around the leviathan, daring each other to touch it until a local teenager, perhaps hoping to impress Marsha, carved a heart in the whale's side with his pocket knife. The three gringo children huddled together, then retreated to their father, who had drawn a little closer and had overseen all this from a dune halfway down from the museum.

Willoughby watched the scene, slightly distracted by the resurrection of a skeleton from his own past that morning. He could see no reason why Yesenia would show up here, when he was trying to reconcile with his wife —

or at least no good reason. He didn't need a scene like this just when Trish was finally starting to trust him again.

Between these concerns and the excitement of the whale, Dan let himself forget about the ATVs they had planned to rent. The kids wanted to race back to the house to tell Trish. It was only a few minutes away, and maybe her nap had refreshed her sufficiently so that she'd come back with them for a quick look before the sun set.

It was nearly six o'clock when Dan Willoughby pulled the family Bronco into the parking space along side his rented beach house. The rental agent had had to give him a map to find it the first time. That had given him a pretty good excuse for not explaining its whereabouts to Yesenia when she'd "accidentally" run into him this morning and asked directions in her half suggestive, half phony-innocent way. Dan didn't need another confrontation like the one Trish and Yesenia had had when Trish barged into Yesenia's apartment in Chandler to call her a whore.

The children raced from the Bronco and into the house while Dan's hand was still mired by sticky thoughts to the steering wheel.

In 1794, the Royal Menagerie in the Tower of London would waive its nine pence admission for visitors willing to donate the family dog or cat and watch their pets fed to the lions. On which side of the wall is the more interesting spectacle? If I were a photographer transported back in time, where would I focus my viewfinder, on the electric-maned carnivore or the upper-class citizens in their enormous, frilled collars? And who would be photographing me?

Siegel

Chapter 4: Then Let Us Go and Make Our Visit

How does one organize an expedition: what equipment is taken, what sources read; what are the little dangers and the large ones? No one has ever written this. The information is not available.

— John Steinbeck, **The Log from the SEA OF CORTEZ.**

When I awake in the spare bedroom of Bev and Don's beach house, I find I'm not all that excited about visiting the actual murder scene. It is a climax coming too soon. What am I going to do next, spend a week searching out local color? I already know the local color: margaritas are dishwater green, the beer is piss yellow.

But it is so quiet early in the early morning. The air in Cholla Bay is clear as a bell, the kind of silence you can't hear in the U.S. At six a.m., one bricklayer with a loud trowel can be cursed by sleeping gringos from miles around.

The next time I wake up, Rex, whom I had no intention of taking with, has come to regale us with stories about how much water his Significant Other Of The Night Before is wasting back at his place. It's only about seven a.m., but something about the muggy heat already in the offing, and the salt air, and maybe Rex, moves me to open a beer.

"Scuba?" Rex inquires.

"Mañana, maybe," I nod.

"Don't worry about the sharks. I've never seen a shark in Cholla Bay. Not one."

Do I want to go scuba diving with an instructor who sees green flashes but doesn't believe in sharks? While I am still considering the possibility that there is a square meter of salt water anywhere in any ocean without a shark in it, Rex begins to argue with Don about the destination of a plane flying overhead at the moment.

"She's bound for Dallas."

"No way, with that trajectory. Houston."

"What movie are they showing?" I ask innocently.

After a brief inventory of my senses, obtaining a report from some internalized Scotty at Damage Control, I decide I can stand getting stinking drunk for a second day in a row. And it's never too early to make a false start; that's what naps are for.

Carole appears on the veranda next to me about a half hour later, by which time I'm holding a coffee in a one hand and a second Tecate in the other, and attempting to vaporize a cloud with my x-ray vision. The beach people are back again too, a gang of them sagging against the hallway around the bathroom, and it's another hour before everybody is ready to go wherever they have to go.

Before I have organized myself, I learn an expedition awaits. My investigation has become a two-vehicle invasion. Carole and I ride with Don, while Rex drives Frenchy and Bev, and, I'm surprised to see, My Imaginary Mistress from the evening before. She is still wearing only an over-sized black t-shirt, but is carrying a camera.

We drive for miles in the sand, Don's hand-held shortwave going crazy all the time with calls for people with handles like "Bushwhacker," "Canadian," and "Mechanic." Then we're into Puerto Penasco itself, where the locals live, the ones who can't even afford to live near the shrimpers and fishing boats that traditionally have been the town's only independent source of income. These poorer folk are part of another ecology altogether, apparently producing a bumper crop of dust this year. The streets are unpaved, and the telephone poles, I'm betting, are just part of the Mexican National Uglification Program, since none of the wires seem to go off into actual homes, and the phones, even those belonging to engineer/handymen such as Don and Rex, rarely seem to work.

We are in this slum, I am informed, to pick up T-Shirt. "T-Shirt?"

"T-Shirt Bob," Don informs me, "but everybody just calls him T-Shirt." Don knows where the Las Conchas development is, but again there are no street names and the house numbers indicate the order in which things were built, not their present topographical relationship to each other. T-Shirt has a variety of gigs going, one of which has something to do with real estate, so he actually knows how to locate the house where the murder occurred.

While I'm trying to evaluate an imaginary individual for whom the name "Bob" must be too formal, this gringo-gone-native who lives down a dirt street cursed with packs of howling dogs and dusty, darting children, the real thing emerges from a house I hadn't suspected of being either inhabited or habitable. He's six-foot-three, with a white beard and a paunch demanding a larger t-shirt than is currently manufactured in these parts. He looks like Hemingway might look after a lobotomy and a year locked up recovering in a bakery. He squeezes in next to me with a roar of greeting and a black cloud of BO that, fortunately, is left in the lurch as the jeep tears off, and chases us ineffectually as long as we keep moving.

I already have told the tale of February 22, 1991, to everyone but T-Shirt, who seems to know it. I am starting to feel like a pervert, and try to convince myself that this telling and retelling is not boorish, but good practice for when (if?) I write the book. But my telling and retelling has created something palpable, as if the words have come out of my mouth in cartoon balloons, balloons then plucked and tied off and paraded around by others, signifying an actual Event In Progress. It has generated a party-like atmosphere, not to mention an anticipation that I know what I'm doing with this investigative reporter thing. No one but me has any doubt that I will deliver the goods for my audience as soon as I get to the murder scene at Number 117 in the Las Conchas development.

Roaring over the jeep racket, T-Shirt in fact directs us to number 117 in the Las Conchas development without missing a pothole. This Number 117 is not quite on the water itself, but is among a row of houses across the ubiquitous sand road from the houses that are. A lot of new development is still going on, and I'm not sure how many of these places have been built since 1991, when the murder occurred. Yet the sand is clean, the ocean bright and blue, the salt air embalming compared to the razor-sharp Arizona desert dryness.

My first thought is simply, why would anyone bring his wife here to this amazingly beautiful, peaceful spot to murder her? The prosecuting attorney, Tom Mitchell, argued at trial that Dan had chosen this place as an isolated locale for the crime. But even in 1991 there were at least a half dozen houses within easy shouting distance of 117. If I wanted isolation for a murder, I might imagine a snow-bound cabin in the woods. This place not only is not isolated, it's too damn sunny.

Am I making sense here? Or does everyone bring his own shade of fantasy to such a place? Maybe Richard Dalmer got up in the morning, heard the birds, smelled the coffee, looked out at the sun, and thought, what a great day to cannibalize some kid. Am I making a mistake by imagining Willoughby thinks or feels like I do, and then discovering, with circular logic, that he is a normal guy?

My troops look at me expectantly, but offer no answers, so I tell Carole, who has volunteered to play shutter-bug, to take a bunch of pictures of this and that. I notice My Imaginary Mistress aping her from behind, so they are like two soldiers on point, covering each other's progress. I jot a few notes on my pad, mostly about how T-Shirt looks this morning. When I can't think of anything else to do, I march up to the front door with Carole and Bev, who is a virtuoso meddler and can pretty much talk anybody into anything.

"Take a picture of that doorknob, will you, Car?" Everyone knows I think the doorknob is terribly important in this investigation.

A nice looking middle-aged lady with a sundress pulled over her tan answers the door. Carole and Bev, both nurses before becoming my assistants this morning, spot her immediately as a doctor's wife with nursing background. There are two little kids standing behind her, so I say tentatively, "Hi, I'm writing a book about ... something that happened in this house a few years ago — "

"Yes, I know about it, but I haven't told the children," she says immediately. Then she lets us come in and snoop all over the place. This writing-a-book thing, I'm discovering, literally opens a lot of doors.

This door opens onto a tiled living room floor, white stucco walls, plenty of windows exposing the southern exposure. There's nouveau rustic furniture and a fireplace to the right of the front door. On the left is the kitchen and dining area. The kids have set up their portable CD player in the living room area while Mom works on lunch.

The murder occurred in one of the two back bedrooms, and the lady who is leasing the house directs us to the right-side room immediately, having this detail from the rental agent. She clearly has imagined the scene and inspected where it happened herself. It's a large room by bungalow standards, with one double bed set against the center of the east wall and a cot pushed up against the north. The floor here too is of large, reddish-brown saltillo tiles. Raw beams hold up the ceiling. A back door, through which Yesenia supposedly entered and left, is on the west wall, and opens out onto a tiny, roofless back porch, an untended area with two rusty chairs and a big flower pot where something in a planter has died. I check out the latch on the back door — it's just one of those hook and eye-screw deals above the kind of door lock even someone like me can open with a credit card or a screwdriver. This is contrary to the prosecutor's claim that a wooden peg pushed down into a slot on the frame would have kept Yesenia from entering had Dan not unhooked it for her after crushing Trish's skull.

The backyard itself is unimproved sand, thirty feet of it in every direction before the next house, the third row back from the beach. The inhabitants of that house not only have to walk further, but they have to look at this shitty back yard. I wonder if this is the house they were building when Yesenia hid her truck behind a big dumpster.

"See a murder weapon?" I ask Carole as we survey the lot.

"I suppose if you made someone eat about a pound of sand."

I look around in particular for places where the murder weapon could have been hidden, even temporarily. According to Yesenia's trial testimony, it was a large metal ball on a rope or chain that Dan put together out of things he picked up at an Army Surplus store. Although it never was found — or even seen — this mace had become a featured part of the prosecution's melodrama, necessary to overshadow the horrifying details of what their star witness, Yesenia herself, admitted to having accomplished in this monastically white room. According to Yesenia, Dan had done the real murder with the mace; her job was only to make it look like an attempted robbery while he was safely away with the children. But the prosecution had never explained what had happened to this absurd, medieval weapon, the kind of thing that surely would have been noticed by a neighbor or a cop. Where could he have flung or buried it that it wouldn't have been noticed when the house was searched? There isn't a shrub in sight, and the ocean is a hundred yards in the other direction through somebody else's yard.

Back inside, Carole and I and sometimes the skinny blonde girl wander around taking notes and pictures of the house, especially the bedroom where the murder occurred, although the blonde's shots seem esoteric in the extreme. After I've observed her taking close-ups of a couple spots on the wall of the Chamber of Horrors, I wait for her to leave, stand aside so there's plenty of light, and stare at the spots. They look completely white to me.

While we're checking out the back door, where Yesenia entered, and the sand dunes behind it, where the murder weapon was never found, we can hear T-Shirt loud-mouthing it up in the kitchen. When I get there, Bev is maintaining the schmooze-level, even while T-Shirt starts to stick his nose into the family breakfast. "What! Your husband's a cardiologist and you're serving him bacon!"

"Well, he's out jogging," the lady explains, clearly getting a kick out of this oddball crew, "clearing a vein or two for it. He drinks red wine too, you know."

"No kidding!" T-Shirt bellows. Bev knows the cardiologist husband's partners, which is not surprising since Bev knows pretty much everybody on the face of the earth who's ever shaken down a thermometer or snapped on a pair of latex gloves.

I run out of things to look at pretty quickly, and eventually herd everyone back outside, especially T-Shirt, who has been sniffing at the cork of the doctor's half-full red wine bottle, and looks ready to take a test-swig. The blonde, who I notice has bits of film negative dangling from her fish hooks, shoots a couple photos of him inhaling critically, and I can hear the lady of the house thinking This One's From Rolling Stone. I get them as far as the front porch, where T-Shirt launches into his rendition of the murder, children or no children. It is clear to him, as it has been to everyone else, that Dan must be guilty of murder because, after all, he fucked a transsexual. When put on the spot, I feel I have to give a brief discourse on how wrong this is. "This doorknob," I say, very authoritatively, "sticks."

The lady looks troubled, as if she's being personally indicted. "Yes, a little. Sometimes a lot, actually."

"That's important. On the morning of the day of the murder, Dan went into town alone, supposedly to check on renting some ATVs to drive on the beach, something a lot of people do even though the use of such vehicles is illegal here."

"My husband complained to the rental agent about the noise," the lady grimaces.

"What the hell did he come down here for?" T-Shirt bellows.

For politeness sake, I pretend T-Shirt is talking about Willoughby. "Well, in the prosecution's version of reality, Dan rented this place just to murder Trish. They say she hated Mexico and he dragged her down here anyway, planning to do the job. But Dan says that she wanted to come, that Trish's brother had been down here and raved about the place, and that's what gave him the idea of presenting the vacation package to her as a gift. Now the ATVs, according to the prosecution, were actually just an excuse for Dan to meet with Yesenia and her brother Tony to go over details of the murder one last time. When Dan returned home, he persuaded the children to go with him to rent the ATVs and to the Cedo, a local museum, while Trish stayed behind to take a nap."

"He killed her," announces T-Shirt.

"Well," I caution, "Marsha said that her Mom originally agreed to go with to the museum and that Marsha herself planned to stay home, so when Willoughby met with Yesenia he wouldn't have known their intended victim was going to stay home. Anyway, as they were leaving the house that afternoon, Dan says he remembered he would need the passports to rent the ATVs, and, leaving the children in the car, he ran back into the house to get them. After waiting for Dan to return for several minutes — somewhere between three and ten, depending on whom you ask — Marsha, who was sixteen, the eldest child, decided to go back into the house after him. But the door wouldn't open immediately. It was either locked or stuck. That's why I asked you about the doorknob. Willoughby comes out a moment later, tucking his white shirt into his pants, and tells Marsha her mother is sleeping and they can get a snack in town. He didn't actually prevent her from entering. Marsha simply agreed and returned to the Blazer with him."

But whether he locked the door, or it stuck, or both of them grabbed it at the same moment could be an important detail.

Everybody agrees that, if Marsha had stepped into the kitchen, she might well have been able to see all the way back to where her mother lay, bashed bloody or settling into the nap she had chosen over the family outing. And that would pretty well have ended this mystery.

Of course I suspect it wouldn't. Marsha, linchpin in the creaking contraption the prosecution has used as Willoughby's death cart, rarely has seemed to be sure of anything. She testified as inconclusively as possible on every occasion. In a post-conviction hearing, she was so obviously ready to perjure herself by recanting her trial testimony that Judge Howe refused to let her testify at all until she was personally represented by an attorney. Nor can one read anything into even this observation. Marsha was not a strong-minded kid to begin with. She'd been a Wednesday's Child, adopted by Dan and Trish just a few years before Trish's murder. At sixteen, Marsha had had no more attentional capacity than Danny, age nine, or Jenny, age seven. Since the murder of her mother, Marsha has been under the dominion of the Huish family, Dan's great antagonists in this whole affair, who had accused him of murdering their daughter before there was the slightest shred of evidence against him. The Huishes personally guided the police on the trail that eventually led to his arrest, and sued him for his wife's entire fortune. At the post-conviction hearing, I saw them, en masse, shuffling awkwardly down the hall of the court building as if they were manacled, laughing about "doing the Danny Walk." Whether or not they intentionally attempted to influence Marsha's testimony, simply being around the Huishes must have had an influence on Marsha.

This is the kind of person, the kind of evidence, on which Dan's life hangs. The only opportunity Dan ever had to kill his wife occurred in that three (or ten) minute interval when he left the kids in the Blazer, supposedly to run back into the house to get the passports he'd forgotten. How long was he really in there? How did he look when he came out? Was the door really locked? How hard did he try to dissuade Marsha from reentering?

I asked Jamie Tepp, the children's babysitter, what she had learned of this from Marsha. "At one point Marsha was hauled in by the police and shown her mother's rings," Jamie told me. "When she got home, she was very, very emotional, and I asked her a few direct questions. . . . I asked her directly to tell me what happened in the time frame of when she got in the van and her dad went back into the house.

"She said they sat there, and then she decided she was hungry and was going to run back into the house. That was not unheard of for these kids. I used to take them to school in the morning, so I know, if you leave them in the car for two minutes, they'll be beeping the horn or getting out of the car and coming in and finding you. So it doesn't surprise me that Marsha found a reason to go back into the house, but the real reason was probably more like, hey, let's get going, than anything else.

"She told me that she walked up to the door and, as she was going to open it, she said there was a tight feeling. She said it was like when you go to open a door and someone has the handle on the other side and you go to turn it and of course they're turning it the other way. She said it was tight. And just then the door opened and her dad was standing there, and he said, `What are you doing?' and she said, `I was going to run in and get a granola bar or something to eat,' something like that. He said, `Well, go ahead, but be quiet because your mom is sleeping.' And Marsha said, `If we're gonna leave now, let's just go,' and they went and got back in the van."

On the doorstep of the rental, I now relate all this. I do it obliquely, so as not to upset the children, who are craning their necks to catch every word and have not been fooled for a second. I am still condensing my canned insights when the surgeon jogs up in a Calvin Klein running rig, pink shorts, blue tank-top, two hundred dollar sneakers with those cute little socks that barely show over the top of the shoes. From twenty yards away I can see the healthy sweat streaking the cultured tan of his face. He slows perceptibly at the sight of a half-dozen strangers cluttering his front steps and making a huge racket.

"How do you like sleeping in a bed where someone murdered his wife?" T-Shirt shouts. The doctor's astonishment makes clear that he has never heard a word about the Famous Crime from his own wife. He hustles the wife and kids back into the house, cutting short T-Shirt's attempt to sell them some rental property. A few minutes later, while we're still horsing around across the street, about to get into our pick-up and jeep, T-Shirt and Don haggling the swap of a long-distance phone call for a loaf of Real Bread from the States, Carole snapping random pictures like a nervous sniper in some advanced position, the blonde covering and advancing with her from a crouch, the doctor reappears on the front porch, wearing a huge scowl and carrying a thick paperback. Apparently he plans to be reading for a while, having just had a huge fight with his wife and gotten himself kicked out of the house on our account. As T-Shirt drives away in Rex's pick-up, on his way to help Jorge empty the vending machines, he shouts back, "Doc, don't forget to wash down that bacon with a big glass of red wine!"

I'm staring across the street now, at the houses lining the beach itself, pretty sure which one had been rented by Dr. Lowry, a GP from Tucson who had been on hand that day in February 1991....

Chapter 5: Telling Stories

Carole says, "Sharing information with people is like giving them a disease." I know what she means, partner.

You may think of *telling a story* as something akin to lying rather than as the very currency of the legal system. Or you may think lies are the very currency. But if you think of "stories" as fiction and legal proof as fact about which lawyers lie, you are wrong on both counts. Stories are how we all make sense of the facts, whether we're putting our kids to bed or trying to keep a client off death row.

Because they are not bored with our wives, our friends don't see our mistresses the way we do. All people, but especially jurors, whose job it is, after all, to be judgmental, will meet a person once and, no matter how unusual the circumstances, form sweeping opinions about them. While Yesenia may not have had the Adam's apple that usually gives away transsexuals, people who met her with Dan were surprised by her.

One: Abe S., one of Dan's oldest friends, was mildly stunned when the two of them showed up on his doorstep in LA one afternoon. Yesenia wore a skin-tight red dress that went about halfway down to her knees, and had on enough makeup to pop out of a Volkswagen for Ringling Brothers. Besides thinking she was a loud-mouthed bimbo, Abe figured there was something else odd about her — a sensation he couldn't shake once he shook her hand. She had a calloused, meaty hand for a woman, he thought.

After explaining to his own wife that, no, Dan hadn't brought Trish this time, Abe took Dan and Yesenia out to a favorite shared pastime at Dodger stadium. While it wasn't Comisky Park, Dan was definitely on one of his "vacations."

It was a beautiful day, and a great game, until a group of teenagers sitting behind them refused to quit smoking the first time Yesenia asked. The kids wouldn't cooperate, and pretty soon she was standing up and shouting at them. "She just stood up and started swearing at them at the top of her voice," Abe recalled. "She was loud-mouthed, and incredibly jealous and aggressive about anything that might affect Dan, like his sinuses in this case. I could see that, before long, she'd be swinging her purse at them. I thought, uh-oh, there go my season tickets, so I moved to the end of the row, out of the way. And I was right. The fists started flying, and Dan and Yesenia and all the kids were ejected from the stadium. They missed a great game."

Two: Yesenia has a history of violence as well as a police record. Her first brush with the law was in 1976, in Woodburn, Oregon, where Yesenia, then Albert Patino, attended the local high school. Responding to a complaint from a local business, undercover police officers set up a sting to catch a young woman who had been soliciting sex on their premises. When an attractive young thing did in fact approach one of the officers with a great deal on a blow job, he counter-offered by telling her she was under arrest, and, as she attempted to turn away, by grabbing her hair. The wig came off in his hands — as the water balloon-filled bra later would. "He was wearing a short skirt and matching heels, full make-up job — had me fooled," the officer reported.

Three: Yesenia was thoroughly capable of imagining threats to Dan as well as to herself in all kinds of situations. Although remarks concerning organized crime families and the mafia are inadmissible in most criminal trials, including Dan's, the prosecution made reference to Dan's "mafia connections" over twenty times during the course of his trial, and got away with it, because attorney Ochoa didn't object even once. There wasn't a shred of evidence to support this alleged connection — except for its assertion by Yesenia. After the trial, she explained that her belief was founded on a single incident at an airport bar. She and Dan were having a drink, when, in the mirror over the bar, Dan spotted two men she'd never seen before. He told her not to look at them, but, after a moment, decided he needed to talk to one of the men by himself. The three men spoke privately for a few minutes, and, when he returned, Dan seemed irritable.

And that was it. Where another woman might have guessed that these two men were acquainted with Trish as well as Dan, perhaps from their church, and so Dan was worried about having been seen with his mistress, Yesenia "naturally" assumed they were mafia.

Four: Yesenia is five-foot-five, 125 pounds, with a thinnish, mischievous face. Although she was born Albert Patino, she was not really "a guy." Yesenia was a rare bird, a true hermaphrodite, born with both male and female sex organs. By high school, Albert's preference became clear, and soon after he/she officially became Yesenia.

In one newspaper photo her hair is dark, worn with bangs in front, long in the back, but piled up on her head to show off the neck, the face. In another, taken after her arrest, the hair has been lightened and cut shorter. People who met her with Dan invariably described her as having "no class," as dressing like a bimbo (or worse). They said she was loud, uncouth, and wore far too much makeup. Yet, in her videotaped deposition, as well as on a number of TV interviews she did with Spanish language stations in Mexico and the United States following her conviction, she dressed relatively conservatively and acted demurely, smiling seriously at times. She resorted apologetically to hand gestures when she feared her generally good English was inadequate, but spoke softly whether she was talking about her family or bludgeoning Trish to death. In the videotape, her apparent normalcy worked to enhance the eerie insanity of what she had to say about the murder.

She said, quite matter-of-factly, that she decided to kill Trish following a confrontation they had over Dan. Trish was not a very confrontational person, but she lost her cool when she learned of the affair. Trish drove to the Windemere Apartments, where Yesenia was living, to have it out. To Trish, it was getting her anger out in the open, releasing it, asserting her position, and moving on. Dan was behaving like a bad boy on summer vacation, but she had no doubt he was hers; he had told her so. This Mexican woman was an insult, an affront, but Dan couldn't seriously be considering leaving his family and home to live in this one bedroom dump with this — whatever she was. She told Yesenia as much.

Because they're often jaded with their husbands as lovers, many wives don't understand that their husbands' mistresses believe themselves to be as loving and as beloved as the wives. As far as Yesenia was concerned, Trish was throwing down the gauntlet. Trish had insulted Yesenia in her own home, had attacked her, because Trish knew that Dan really loved her and not Trish. And Yesenia was not going to give up a fight she believed she was winning because of some gringo lady's threats. I will take your man, and your family, and your house, Yesenia swore. One way or another.

From Caborca prison, where she is serving a 35-year sentence for murder, Yesenia reports this, and much, much more quite matter-of-factly. The only questions that seem to break her calmness and self-possession concern whether Dan really loved her. To this day she does not doubt it, although he has not written or spoken to her since she testified at his trial. And she understands that, too. Her videotaped confession is not so much a peace offering to a man she has wronged as it is a love offering to a man she wants to win back.

Four disjointed anecdotes about a woman's life: the first, the mildly comic baseball incident, is designed to make you see Yesenia, as Abe did, with distaste and a foreshadowing of her violence; the story of her first arrest, which comes next, provides official confirmation of her lawlessness; the third, her "mafia story," illustrates her propensity to become completely convinced by her own extreme fantasies; by the fourth anecdote, the reader should be ready to accept the idea that Yesenia is quite likely to have believed that Dan was far more devoted to her than he really was, and that, in her twisted mind, killing Trish to secure Dan for herself was not just appropriate, but obvious.

Scientific research on transsexuals does not make them out to be more inclined to violence than anyone else. Clearly, however, if you're going to have this kind of surgery, you are far more prone than I am to extreme actions based on self-image. How else can one even contemplate this kind of surgery? The conventional "true murder" story or forensic study would suggest this mad transsexual is the logical suspect in the planning and murder of Trish, while nothing in Dan's background points even to his awareness of her intent, much less his complicity. If we can forgive Clinton for jeopardizing the security of the free world for a blow job, if we can seriously doubt O.J.'s guilt, for even a fraction of a second, how can we blame Dan for not seeing what, in hindsight, he might have seen, namely that his lover was mad enough and possessive enough to kill his wife? After all, his lust for her was so great that he never even suspected she had started life as a man, a fact his more objective friend Abe came close to intuiting on their first meeting — without making love to her.

And Dan believed this even though he knew Bonus Story Number Five:

Dan had thought Jack Mielke, Yesenia's former husband, was relatively friendly. When I asked Dan why, then, Mielke would testify against him, my suspicion was that it was because Mielke still loved Yesenia and would do whatever he could to protect her. But Dan's answer was: "Blackmail."

Nothing like living on death row for a few years to twist your thinking into a wet towel of paranoia you snap at everything that goes by. "The A.G. is blackmailing both of them. Mielke is blackmailing Yesenia to keep her in line," Dan clarifies. Snap, snap.

But it's not what I think. Dan tells me this story:

When Yesenia and Mielke were married, they lived in Mexico. Things weren't going great between them after a while, because, guess what, they're pretty fucked up people. So what do they decide to do to save the marriage? Adopt a child. Brilliant. And no one is going to let them adopt, so instead Mielke goes out and buys a baby. I think he paid like $2,000. They call him Charlie. But guess what, things don't get any better between them. Yesenia is out cruising the bars, and one night she lets herself be picked up by these three off-duty Federales. They ask her if she wants to go to a party with them, but instead they take her out into the jungle and rape her. Yesenia comes home, all beat up, but won't tell Mielke what happened. Instead, when she gets better, she puts on a blond wig, what she considers a disguise, and her and a girlfriend go cruising those same bars looking for the Federales. One night she finds two of them. They let themselves be talked into the same "let's go *to this party" scam, but when the Federales drive them out into the jungle to rape them, Yesenia pulls out this .38 she stole from Mielke and shoots one of them right in the chest. The other one gets away. Her and the girlfriend dump the body over a cliff, and drive home.*

She's so proud of herself, of course she tells Mielke about it that night. He freaks completely. Federales may be mean, corrupt bastards, but they're still cops. He sees the ballistics test tying him to the gun. Just possessing a handgun in Mexico gets you thrown in jail. In this case, however, Mielke figures he's either going to be tortured to death or spend the rest of his life in a Mexican jail. So he takes the gun and baby Charlie and he and Yesenia pile into the camper and emigrate, unofficially, back to the U.S. They have no passport for Charlie, and only a fake one for Yesenia, so they hide Charlie under some blankets and get him across that way.

He's been in the US illegally ever since. That's where the blackmail comes in. The AG's Office knows Charlie will be deported if they tell Immigration. They've raised him like a regular kid. He lives with Mielke in Sedona. So the AG can get Mielke to say whatever they want. And Yesenia, just in case she doesn't already have enough reasons to cooperate, is being blackmailed by Mielke with the gun. He keeps it in a safety deposit box and threatens her with it when she gets out of line. If he turned it over now, while she's already in custody in Mexico, she'd never get out of that jail alive.

Snap. Snap. Snap... ?

Telling the story is what trials are all about. People instinctively understand reality by imagining events in story form. When only pieces of information are available, we have to imagine the missing pieces to complete a scene. We would hope that, when a man's life hangs in the balance, the missing pieces are relatively few and the final picture irrefutably clear. Unfortunately, the process more often resembles reconstructing the mythology of Orion from a handful of stars that look like a belt to the guy closest to the campfire.

After he chooses and works up the rough draft of his scenario from the preliminary facts, a lawyer and his investigators go back out into the field to pull together as much evidence as possible to confirm his version of reality. At best, he hopes to fit new dots of information into the visualized pattern. I hope that is what I am doing in Mexico. Because at worst, the lawyer will avoid, ignore, or downplay things he discovers that do not fit. Willoughby is in jail because the prosecution did that, and because his defense failed to tell the other side of the story.

Prosecutors and police officers both have a duty to tell the truth, and that includes divulging any contrary evidence that turns up in the course of an investigation. I think most people involved in the justice system take that duty seriously. But there's a terrific temptation to bury bits of information that don't fit your version. If contrary evidence can be explained away somehow, for instance as the delusional confession of an already condemned killer, then why should the agent of justice confuse the scenario and make a jury's task more difficult by repeating a patently absurd tale?

One reason they have to is that the prosecution has a duty to share evidence that might prove the innocence of a defendant, under a United States Supreme Court case called **Brady v. Maryland**. In **Brady**, the Supreme Court said state prosecutors violated a homicide defendant's constitutional right to a fair trial by withholding the transcript of an interview in which the prosector's key witness himself confessed to the murder. Brady was granted a new trial.

In Willoughby's case, the prosecution has been accused of a number of Brady violations. For instance, they apparently interviewed the insurance agent who sold Trish and Thera a $750,000 "key-man" life insurance policy for their business, hoping to shore up their theory that Dan was motivated by money to murder his wife. Killing for profit is one way of only a few ways to earn the death penalty in Arizona. The insurance agent told Debra Schwartz, an investigator for the prosecutor's office, that not only did Dan not know about the insurance, but that Thera Huish had asked him to lie about it and had filed a false complaint with the Department of Insurance when he had refused. Because the agent's testimony might have exonerated Willoughby, the prosecutors had a duty to tell David Ochoa, Dan's lawyer, about their interview. They never did, and Ochoa, being incompetent, never interviewed the man himself.

When, at Willoughby's hearing for a new trial, Judge Howe asked Investigator Schwartz about her failure to make a report on this interview and turn the information over to the defense, she claimed that the purpose of her visit to the insurance agent was merely to pick up certain documents, and that she had no recollection of talking with him.

Along with Kay Lines, Debra Schwartz also was involved in interviewing a witness directed to the A.G.'s Office by the Gilbert Police Department. Lines had commandeered the Gilbert police, as he had those of Chandler and Mesa, other southeastern suburbs of Phoenix, to do legwork, although he refused to allow them to develop any of their own leads.

On the morning of June 21, 1991, with Yesenia supposedly hiding out in Mexico and the identity of any accomplices still supposedly at issue, a Gilbert Police Detective named Randy McLaws received a tip that Yesenia had been spotted in Mesa. McLaws went to the residence of Lona Mason, who had been Yesenia's neighbor about three years earlier. Lona told McLaws that she had seen Yesenia just two days before at a local grocery store. According to Lona, Yesenia had been accompanied by a stocky white male of German descent, forty to forty-five years old, with short blond graying hair. The man, whom Lona knew only as "George," was driving a "beer bottle brown" BMW. Yesenia told Lona that George was her ex-husband, currently working at a resort in Sedona where he lived with their "son" Benjamin. Lona knew Yesenia couldn't have biological children, so assumed this son was the adopted Hispanic child Yesenia also called "Bajeo," who had played with her own children when they'd been neighbors. Lona had seen photos of Yesenia, George, and Bajeo together in the past.

When Lona asked Yesenia what she was doing these days, Yesenia told her they were just stopping in town to score some cocaine on their way from Sedona to Mexico City. George was visibly upset by her candor, and Yesenia made Lona swear not to tell anyone she'd seen them, not even Lona's own husband.

Lona told McLaws that she'd never met Dan Willoughby, but had heard Yesenia talk about him the year before. Yesenia had said she loved Dan and would do "anything" for him. Dan had been good to her, had never beaten her as prior lovers had, and "had lots and lots of money." A few months before Trish's murder, Yesenia had come by with t-shirts for Lona's kids she'd just purchased in Rocky Point. "If his wife wasn't around, we could be together," Yesenia had said.

Lona knew a great deal about Yesenia. She told McLaws her favorite restaurants and hangouts, including her favorite Victoria's Secrets. (Yesenia, who sometimes went by the name Victoria Mielke, once told Lona, "You'd be amazed at how many Victorias have secrets.") One of Yesenia's secrets was that she was a devout member of the Santaria Cult, a religion based on blood sacrifice. Yesenia always carried a sacrificial knife with her.

McLaws concluded his report with the observation that "George" shared many similarities with George "Jack" Mielke, Yesenia's ex-husband, with whom she had apparently adopted a Hispanic son of the correct age. He not only fit Lona's physical description, but worked at a resort in Sedona. He also drove a brown BMW.

McLaws then obtained a photo of Jack Mielke and showed it to Lona, who immediately identified him as "George." She also identified a photo of the son, known to police only as "Charlie," and confirmed several times that she was "100% sure" about both identifications. McLaws immediately passed on all this information to the Attorney General's Office.

The AG's Office filed a very different report. It says that, on June 26, Schwartz and Lines conducted their own half-hour follow-up interview. Startlingly, in their interview, Lona supposedly identified "George" as Dan Willoughby, the man she'd told McLaws she'd never met. Schwartz's report indicates that Lona tried to tell her "other things" about Yesenia's "bi-sexual and transsexual friends and drugs," yet reports specifically only one item, unrelated to the murder case, which Schwartz "knew" to be false.

Neither side ever spoke to Lona Mason again. Mielke went on to give very damaging testimony against Dan at trial.

Dan's attorney, David Ochoa, ignored these reports, like so many others, "to save Dan money" on the investigation. That Mason might, with one stone, have discredited both of the prosecution's star witnesses as co-conspirators apparently wasn't even worth a phone call.

The behavior of the AG's investigators is just as peculiar. Even their own report indicates Mason was offering them leads that might have helped locate Yesenia, their primary investigative goal at that time, yet they made no notes of her information. Their report also indicates they did not show Mason a photo of Mielke, but only one of Willoughby, who did not have a German accent, did not fit the description of "George," did not drive a brown BMW, did not live in Sedona, and did not have a child with Yesenia. Certainly the discrepancy between these two identifications was worth a second look. No one took it.

Perhaps Ochoa, out of laziness and credulity, was anxious to believe that Lona Mason would not make a credible witness, as the AG's report implied. Perhaps he entertained a suspicion that his own client's protestations were false, that Dan and not Jack Mielke was "George."

But if anyone was really going to believe that Dan might have been with Yesenia after her fingerprints confirmed her as Trish's murderer, it would have been the AG's office. Why not follow up and call Mason as a witness who could support their allegation that Willoughby had conspired with Yesenia all along? Instead, the AG's report seems patently designed to excuse any further pursuit of any of the information offered by Mason, to obscure the truth by dismissing an unfavorable witness as unreliable.

It bugs the hell out of me when characters in a mystery or suspense story fail to follow up on obvious leads that might solve crimes or save lives. Usually I assume that the writer just can't think of a better way to attenuate the action, and that, in real life, both prosecutors and defendants would have tagged all these obvious bases before racing for home. For this reason, the Lona Mason interview disturbed me a lot. Hell, I thought, and opened the phone book. She must have disappeared or refused to cooperate; otherwise someone would have spoken to her for sure in the past seven years.

Not many single women are listed by their full names in the phone book. I'm used to looking for all kinds of variations, and sometimes get Grave Danger involved.

But there she was. I called. She'll never talk to me, I thought, or she'll want money, or her brain will be pickled in drugs and alcohol.

Lona Mason sounded cheery and anxious to help, and remembered the McLaws interview pretty clearly without prompting on my part. Except for a few omissions, the product of the interceding seven years, she repeated the exact same information I had read on the report, including all the details of Mielke's description. He had had a slight German accent, she thought.

"If you were her friend, why did you report her to the police?" I asked, mindful that people have a tendency to turn their personal facts to better face an important event in order to bask in reflected glory.

"Oh, I didn't think she did it," Mason told me. "She was always really nice around me." Lona had never heard a word about the case afterwards, and hadn't been aware until my phone call of the nature of the evidence against Yesenia or that Dan Willoughby was on death row. She and Yesenia had had adjoining apartments and shared a balcony, where they used to sunbathe together. Yesenia's only obvious shortcoming was with men. She lied to them a lot, manipulated them a lot, and was good at it, and got herself in trouble by two-timing them a lot. "That's why her Mexican boyfriend--what's his name?--beat her up."

"Able Rascon?" Yesenia married this younger man after she divorced Jack Mielke. Currently he was in prison on a drug conviction.

"Yeah, that sounds right. He found out George was here whenever he was gone, so he beat her up. Then I never saw him, that Able guy, again."

"But you liked her?"

"Yeah. She was extremely likeable. Maybe it was partly because she was such a good liar. She'd draw you in, and, then by the time you figured out what she was up to, she'd disappeared. It's not her fault, you know what I mean? It's just how she was. How she was made. We kept in touch, on and off, for years after she'd moved out. I liked her."

"And she never mentioned Dan to you?"

"Not much. I think she said a couple times she had this new boyfriend, Dan, who was a really nice guy."

"Did she mention he had a lot of money?" I asked, glancing at the McLaws report.

"Probably," Lona laughed. "Money was a major item for her. She liked to spend it. Not that I was a slouch. I was married to a drywall contractor in those days."

"What I can't figure out," I said, "is the apparent contradictions between what you've told me and Detective McLaws and what's in the second police report, the one based on the interview you gave to the Attorney General's Office."

There was silence for a moment. "What second report?"

"The one you gave to the two investigators from the AG's office a few days after you talked to the Gilbert police detective. A man named Kay Lines and a woman named Deborah Schwartz."

"I never spoke to those people. I never gave a second interview."

"You don't remember them coming to talk to you and showing you a picture of Dan Willoughby? According to them, you identified him as the `George' you'd seen with Yesenia."

"How could I have? I've never met Dan Willoughby. And I never saw a photo of him except maybe one in the newspaper. I saw that George at least a half-dozen times."

"You're telling me you're certain you didn't talk to two investigators from the AG's office? A man and a woman. Just a few days after the first interview."

"Except for the one cop from Gilbert, I never spoke to anyone about this, not for seven years, until you called."

"But," I said slowly, trying not to rush to the kind of conclusions we're allowed to rush to in novels, "that would mean the police lied on purpose to convict Dan. To put a man on death row with lies, that's harsh. That's hard to accept."

"Not for me," Lona snorted. "I dated a cop."

All I was looking to give you was a good example of a Brady violation, and now there's this.

In his **Atlantic Monthly** article "The Wrong Man," Alan Berlow reports that, since 1976, more than eighty death row inmates have had their convictions reversed. This may seem like a reasonable price to pay for a justice system that works "most of the time," until you realize this is about 15% of the number of people actually executed in the United States during that period. Since 1963, when **Gideon v. Wainright** required states to provide some form of legal defense to poor defendants accused of serious crimes, at least 381 homicide convictions have been overturned because prosecutors concealed evidence of a defendant's innocence or presented evidence they knew to be false. Berlow describes at some length the case of Rolando Cruz, who spent over ten years on death row after being branded a child murderer and sodomist, in a case where there was no direct evidence against him, where another man, already convicted of raping and murdering another young girl, had confessed to the murder, and where DNA evidence had essentially eliminated Cruz even as a possible suspect. After three trials, police finally admitted to lying under oath to secure Cruz's conviction.

Often people who are critical of what they believe to be the vast array of legal protections for the accused and convicted do not realize that there is virtually no other safeguard except the freeing of a suspect for prosecutorial misconduct to prevent cases like Cruz's. Only once in American legal history have prosecutors and investigators actually been indicted for purposefully hiding evidence that proved a defendant's innocence or falsifying evidence or using evidence they knew to be false, and those charges were later dismissed. The reason is partly that the standard of proof for prosecutorial misconduct is extremely high so that honest prosecutors will not be deterred from vigorously pursuing convictions in an adversarial justice system. (Unfortunately, this is precisely the scare tactic used by prosecutors in the Willoughby case when they terrorized his defense attorney with threats of criminal prosecution if witnesses were interviewed out of their presence.) And let's face it: prosecutors are not going to prosecute each other for excessive zeal. As Berlow points out, it already is a poorly kept secret that witnesses, including convicted criminals, who lie under oath for the state will never be prosecuted for perjury, while those who testify for defendants may be threatened with perjury at all phases of a trial.

Nor is there any civil remedy for wrongly convicted defendants. For all practical purposes, it is impossible to sue the state for wrongful conviction, because the wrongly convicted man must prove he was prosecuted out of "malice" rather than any belief in his guilt. Nor do most states provide any compensation for victims of wrongful convictions, and those that do tend to be merely token repayments. Arizona offers no compensation at all. If Dan Willoughby ever walks away from his conviction, he will do so completely destitute, ten years of his life and his business career gone, and the state will merely shrug its huge metaphorical shoulders.

While I repeatedly have confessed to being a natural skeptic, it is because I find that nothing breeds paranoia like reality. One might expect the Supreme Court to give a balanced report of the facts of the Willoughby case, but judges too are anxious to tell the story in the way that best supports their final judgment. So, as soon as misstatements of fact and chronology became obvious to me, I doubted the veracity of everything in their authoritative summary.

Even a completely honest writer or a lawyer may save certain bits of information to reveal at a dramatic moment, but I do not want to be guilty of hiding any of the facts of the Willoughby story, no matter how contradictory. And I also wrestle with the further temptation to interpret what I see in an intellectually honest way, without putting a self-serving spin on the facts the way I would be allowed to when telling a story in court. For instance, a Dr. Harold Lowry and his family occupied the vacation home across the street from the Willoughbys, and Dr. Lowry eventually testified at trial concerning his observations of Willoughby and the crime scene. In particular, he testified that Willoughby was behaving oddly, that he seemed far less concerned about his wife than about the police who arrived to investigate. Lowry is not a psychiatrist, but, the prosecution will argue, his medical practice has given him the opportunity to observe hundreds of people in crisis. If the jury likes and trusts Lowry, they will be concerned about Willoughby's inappropriate behavior. So I've tried to imagine Lowry in a way that made his testimony relatively harmless to Willoughby:

Harold Lowry was having dinner, the steak and eggs he'd insisted his wife bring with them from the States, in stark contrast to the Mexican-style dining room of his rented beach house, to the sound of surf just outside the room. Lowry frowned: the surf sounded as if it were getting closer. Was the tide going out or coming in? As a physician, he was used to finding answers to his own questions. He could tell it was either high or low tide by looking at the rank green seaweed at his doorstep, but could he tell if the tide was coming or going by the way the waves were shaped? Scientific method would require the skinny-legged Lowry to stand at the shoreline in bare feet for at least several minutes while the waves lapped further and further in around his ankles or receded from his inquiring toes in order to answer this question — a question, in truth, with which he only preoccupied himself in order to keep his mind off the absence of air conditioning in this place, in this expensive holiday beach house. If he thought about the sound of the waves he wouldn't miss the hum of air conditioning.

Suddenly another sound shattered the silence of Lowry's dinner table. His wife was more startled than he. It was as if he had started a conversation for once.

He was almost comforted by the familiar noise. To the Tucson physician, ambulance sirens registered somewhere between the sound of incoming artillery to a soldier and the sound of milk-sodden cows complaining to a farmer.

Instinctively Lowry responded to the familiar call. His wife detected his faint smile of almost sexual gratification as he pushed back from the table and hurried from the room, and from the vacation she had so painstakingly planned.

The ambulance was parking right across the street, at that older, cheaper-looking house with the three noisy kids. The vehicle was one of those white jobs, of course, with a couple of red crosses, the ones that were always begging money from the tourists. The attendants, themselves no more than a couple of kids who had been issued uniforms that made them look like they worked in a car wash, were pulling medical bags from the back of their vehicle with no more haste than Lowry might have expected from these people. He shuddered to think what they might do if that equipment was actually needed.

Fortunately, by the time Lowry made it across the street, there was a middle-aged Anglo with longish but well-trimmed hair and wire-rimmed glasses, an American, Lowry assumed, standing in the doorway of the house. "Can I help?" Lowry asked professionally. "I'm a doctor."

The man appeared to stare at him in disoriented shock, as if the possibility of speaking with someone in his own language came as a remarkable surprise. The illusion was shattered a moment later when the man spoke quickly in Spanish to the ambulance attendants before turning back to Lowry. It was a strange combination of alarm and efficiency that the physician found odd in anyone outside of his own profession. "My wife. In there," he gestured to Lowry.

Lowry went through the front door of the beach house. It wasn't as sumptuous as his own, of course. The first room was a combination kitchen and living room that spanned the entire twenty-five-foot width of the building. Next to the fireplace in the far corner of the room, the three children sat in tortured silence. An older one who didn't look biologically related — perhaps an au pair? — huddled the other two under her arms. Two hallways led back to the rest of the house. Lowry followed the man's gesture into the hallway on the right.

Lowry was anticipating a good old-fashioned heart attack. Cardiology wasn't his specialty, of course, but there was no doubt he was the best bet this woman would have if she was in a life-threatening situation. There was no hospital in town, and the clinic barely had electricity. Staff parking was a bicycle rack, for Christ's sake!

The doorway at the end of the hallway that Lowry entered was only ten feet away, but it separated him from the reality he had anticipated by miles.

As Willoughby's defender, this is a version of events I can live with. My unsympathetic portrait of the doctor neutralizes his subjective observations concerning Dan's reactions, which a juror will accept only insofar as she accepts the doctor himself.

I need to work with the evidence at hand. All of it is purely circumstantial. Lowry's testimony about Willoughby "acting strangely" might not even have been allowed if Dan had had a decent lawyer. Lowry was just speculating — and, let's face it, who would be acting "normally" if he just found his wife floating in a pool of blood? On the other hand, if such evidence did come in, it could be particularly damaging. While few people know much about DNA evidence and are skeptical of anything about which two experts can argue ad nauseam, most of us feel comfortable with evaluating human behavior. We expect people to react in a certain way, and when they don't, we want to know why. A number of witnesses claiming that John Henry Knapp acted peculiarly on the morning his daughters burned to death were instrumental in his (later overturned) convictions.

The thing is, I've interviewed Dr. Lowry, and he seems like a really nice guy. All the snide, prejudicial little details I've built into my story, while technically no more or less significant than his own analysis of Willoughby, are not based on my own sense of the doctor.

If I presented this version of him to you, I'd be committing my own sort of Brady violation. For Dan's sake, I'd be better off not getting to know Lowry any better. Otherwise, my story might have to read more like this:

Dr. Harold Lowry was halfway through the dinner he'd helped his wife prepare when the ambulance siren wailed up the street outside. He reacted instinctively.

"Hal," his wife looked at him hopefully. "You don't have to. You're on vacation."

That was true enough, he supposed. His family practice in Tucson afforded Lowry neither the vacation time nor the money available to some other doctors. He told himself that the fulfillment of being able to help whole families stay healthy by practicing general medicine was a more than sufficient trade-off, but it didn't do much to compensate his own family.

But then the ambulance stopped at the house right across the street. "It's that new family," he told his wife as he got up from the table. "That family from Phoenix with the three kids. I'd better check, just to make sure they don't need emergency help. There may not be a medical doctor for miles."

By the time he got across the street, the Mexican ambulance attendants were hauling a stretcher through the front door, past the man of the house. The man's complexion was none too good, and Hal made a note to check him out after he found out where the emergency was. "I'm an MD," he said, extending his hand. "Hal Lowry."

The man stared at him strangely, neither returning the hand shake nor stepping out of the door way.

"What's going on?" Lowry asked. "Maybe I can help."

Reluctantly, the man moved aside and pointed into the house. "In there. My wife."

Lowry stepped into the living room/kitchen that made up the big front room of the house, then followed the excited voices of the ambulance attendants down the hallway to the right. He didn't need to speak Spanish to understand the urgency of their tone.

But he wasn't ready for what he saw, anymore, apparently, than had been the three young men with the stretcher. They were simply staring in shock at the woman practically floating in her own blood on the bed. She was lying face-up with what looked like a kitchen knife protruding from her temple. A similar knife, blade bent, was lying on the floor next to the bed.

Just then the woman gasped. She was alive, but probably drowning in her own blood. Lowry pushed the men aside and began to check her respiration. Someone had placed a bath towel, now completely soaked in blood, over the top of her face and head, and when he lifted it he saw what he had already expected. The knife was barely hanging from the scalp, the stabber unable to penetrate the thick skull with its point. The real damage had been done by some blunt object, and there seemed to be a lot of it, at least six or seven indentations suggesting substantial cranial fractures.

Lowry did what he could to stanch her loss of blood. She was middle-aged and apparently had been healthy. Her only hope rested on his getting her to an advanced medical facility as soon as possible. He supervised the attendants, then followed them out of the bedroom with their loaded stretcher. When he got back to the living room and saw the children, huddled together around the fire place, the full horror of the scene finally hit him. These kids had been the ones to find their mother like that.

Lowry ran back across the street and got his wife. In a dozen words, he explained what had happened and brought her back with him to care for the children. By that time the ambulance was loaded and ready to leave.

The husband was still standing in the doorway, looking at neither the kids nor the ambulance, but off down the road somewhere. "Are you all right?" Lowry asked him.

"Uh, yeah. I guess so," Willoughby answered.

"The ambulance is leaving," the doctor pointed out. "Don't you want to go with your wife? She's still alive. But she'll have to be air-evaced to Tucson, or at least Hermosillo." Lowry had heard something about the Mexican government forbidding American medical copters to land here, but there seemed no point in going into that now.

The man gave him a confused — and confusing — look.

Lowry said, "Look, they're already leaving. You can follow them in your Blazer here, but you'd better get going. I couldn't understand where they're taking her."

"But my children. And the police... ."

"My wife will take care of the kids. She's a nurse. She can handle it."

"The police — I better stay and talk to them."

"I'm sure you can do that later. Go on. I'll tell them you went with your wife. I'm sure they'll understand. Hurry, the ambulance will be out of sight in a minute."

Lowry watched Dan Willoughby get in the Blazer and back out of the drive. By the time he'd reached the gate of Los Conchas estates in pursuit of the ambulance, the police cars passed him, heading toward the house.

Damn, thought Lowry, as he watched the Blazer turn around and head back to the house, what the hell is wrong with that guy? But then, he thought, who knew what anybody would do in a crisis, except probably fuck up.

Dan Willoughby says Dr. Lowry testified pretty much on the money except for his recollection of Dan's failure to follow Trish's ambulance. According to Dan, he was eager to follow the ambulance, and did so as soon as Mrs. Lowry had taken the kids across the street, but was forced to turn around and go back to the house by police who arrived at that point to investigate. Dan protested that he would be unable to find the hospital if he didn't go with the ambulance, and the police finally agreed to send an officer with him to show him the way after Dan let them back into the house.

Perhaps the greatest irony of judicial storytelling is that the irrelevant or untrustworthy elements of the story may be most influential with the jury. (If such elements favor the other side, lawyers argue they are "more prejudicial than probative" to get them excluded under a rule of evidence.) Let's say that you find Dr. Lowry as charming and open as I did. Does Dr. Lowry's pleasantness mean he is right in his perplexity about Willoughby's behavior? Of course not. In what might be called the Quantum Theory of Evidence, a corollary to Heisenberg's Uncertainty Principle, what a witness has to say about an event changes the moment he is asked to give testimony. Imagine yourself as a witness who is told that your observations are crucial in proving that a man is guilty of a terrible crime. Suddenly, events that had little or no particular significance are spotlighted; now you see them in a new way. No matter how impartial you are, you cannot help but see these events differently than you saw them before they were illuminated in this manner. Every detail that might be significant now casts a long shadow. If the testimony you give concerns an overt physical action, such as whether Dan Willoughby shook your hand, an honest person with a sound memory will be able to say yes or no. But the questions will continue: was his palm sweaty, his grip firm? While still dealing with the overtly physical, not just a finer memory than most of us possess but *interpretation* is now implicit in your answer. Perhaps you didn't question his grip at the time, not seeing perspiration as an index of character. Many people have sweaty hands because of the heat or glandular conditions. So your memory strains, trying to remember if the palm was a little sweaty or a lot sweaty, trying to judge for yourself whether the medium amount of sweat you think you recall fell on one side of the line or the other.... A man's life is at stake, a woman's honor, her family's justice. Are you going to tell these people you won't answer the question because you're not positive or you don't think this handshake was significant? If you do, they'll ask the question again, in a slightly different way, and again....

I wish witnesses such as Dr. Lowry could be spared this dilemma. Objective witnesses with the courage to step forward and volunteer what they know are absolutely essential to justice. But knowing what you know is not always a simple matter.

Siegel

Chapter 6: Guilt

Rex and Frenchy and the beach people are milling around Bev's kitchen.

"So, is he guilty?" Bev asks as she hands me a gin and tonic.

"Absolutely," Carole announces from her side.

Either of them might mean me, but I choose to believe we're talking about my scapegoat.

"He didn't get a fair trial." That's the one thing in this case I am sure about. "His lawyer was completely incompetent. The guy had been dressed down by the State Supreme Court the year before — in print! — for ineffectiveness in another criminal case. He didn't cross-examine the witnesses properly." I'm uncomfortable with my theatrical outrage, but am determined to do my best for the sake of the story. "He didn't present a defense, because, he said, he was sure Willoughby's case would be dismissed on jurisdictional grounds. Which is dumb: the murder was committed in Mexico, but Willoughby was accused of conspiring up in Phoenix."

"Why didn't Willoughby fire him?" Bev obliges me by asking. Maybe Carole is silent because she's heard all this; maybe she has other reasons.

"I think he wanted to believe in the guy. Ochoa was a Hispanic, had a reputation in the Hispanic community."

"Now he's selling real estate," Don observes.

"Is Willoughby Hispanic?" Bev asks.

"No, but —"

"Yesenia is," Carole interjects, puncturing the ascending balloon of the lecture I have prepared on Hispanophilia as a particularly Southwestern liberal guilt trip, with a sidebar on **The Heart of Darkness**. I deliver an abbreviated version as she wanders off.

Like other survivors from the Sixties, Willoughby loved all things Mexican. The country was a mythological repository for the imagined potentialities of his youth, for the possibilities for freedom that seemed to exist back in that decade when our own authorities stumbled, cracked, appeared briefly vulnerable — before the armies of darkness regrouped and, while we were stoned, overran our cinder-block-and-milk-crate barricades, fouled our tie-died t-shirts, and made off with the only women in the world who believed in free love. But in the jungles of Mexico, both natural and urban, outlaw souls still roamed without neckties and taxes, keeping the faith the rest of us pretend not to have lost but merely misplaced. Perhaps this is why Dan was so easily captivated by Yesenia, a Mexican, although she was even more exotic than he first imagined. In their affair, he must have sensed her wildness, her foreignness deep and dense and aswarm with secrets. What else did he know?

But Carole's point is clear: Can he be guiltless for not imagining the monsters you catch when you bait your trap in the jungle?

Never having fully believed in the Sixties, even as my own long hair flew in the vanguard of student demonstrations, red bandanna shading eyes bloodshot from pot, I imagine myself somewhat less naive about what Mexico really is, although I am simply more pessimistic. Which means, as Frenchy and I sip our beers and stare thoughtfully from the concrete veranda in front of the suddenly empty beach house, that my eyes wander down to the shore, scanning the young bodies dancing among the waves. There is an occasional thunk as someone blasts away at the tide with a home-made potato launcher constructed of PVC and powered with little cans of propane. Frenchy asks the obvious question. "So why are they after him if he didn't do nothin'?"

"I think they got their version of reality from the mother-in-law, Thera Huish. She had plenty of reasons for wanting Willoughby convicted. And it was convenient for the Attorney General's Office to believe her. Just a few months before Trish Willoughby was killed, Arizona investigators caused an uproar by bungling the investigation of the Temple Murders. Remember them?"

Frenchy nodded in recollection of the spectacular atrocity. In that case, nine Buddhist acolytes were shot execution-style in the community kitchen of their monastery in a Phoenix suburb. In response to the public outcry, Maricopa County sheriff's deputies rounded up several suspects and interrogated them illegally in a hotel room for several days until they obtained signed confessions — which subsequently proved to be false.

"The same month, the AG's Office was reversed on a big-deal conviction of another guy, John Henry Knapp. He supposedly burned up his daughters in a garage blaze. The Court of Appeals ruled the conviction had been obtained by suppressing evidence against his wife, the State's prime witness, who is now suspected to have been the actual murderer." I went on. Eight state legislators had been indicted in a bribery scam. Charles Keating, a Phoenix local with strong ties to state politicos, had been convicted of fraud in the collapse of Lincoln Savings & Loan, his crimes resulting in a U.S. Senate Ethics Committee probe of both Arizona Senators. The Governor himself was indicted in a $140 million law suit by the RTC. A Superior Court Judge was suspended after his second arrest for drug possession. And the state police were tagged with a half million dollar judgment for negligently shooting to death a teenage suspect while he already was in custody.

"I think this is why Arizona authorities were more interested in nailing Willoughby than in accepting Yesenia as the murderer, like the Mexican police. Dan Willoughby must have looked like an image fix for the prosecutor's office."

Frenchy thinks about this, and does not ask whether I think Willoughby is guilty anyway. I have not spoken up with my own most intimate thoughts on Willoughby's guilt. Perhaps Frenchy knows I have not even posed the obvious questions. Who among us has not had an affair? How much did we know of our lovers before we took that plunge? Who has not fought, has not used words he later regretted, or even physical violence? These are not questions for tourists.

Carole has wandered off during my familiar diatribe. I find her complaining to Bev about Rex, or maybe me, and Bev apparently has offered some lame excuse on his, or my, behalf. "Fuck that," Carole says. "I know all about human nature. That doesn't mean I have to accept it."

As if on cue, Rex appears to tell Carole that tonight's green flash was particularly vivid, and she gives his back a murderous look, almost deranged in its intensity.

There are fires on the beach, one of which must be that of My Imaginary Mistress. Who is she with? Some lean teenage boy whose weight could be carved from my side and still leave an entire old man behind? It seems somehow unfair that she is able to enter our world, to study and observe us, while we are left only to fantasize about hers. While I am left to fantasize. Maybe if I had run away from my home as a youth and spent a year living on Mexican beaches, without money or clothing or a bed — or had I traveled in Europe, like Dan — I would understand a little better, I would not envy her lack of baggage so much, would give more weight to the sweat, and hunger, and fear that is a part of her scene.

Is there some sort of Warholian promise that we all will get fifteen minutes of freedom in our lives? Willoughby must have believed something like that when, on the spur of an impulse, he picked up Yesenia at the bus stop in front of a Circle K and discovered this exotic Mexican beauty was willing to flirt with an average-looking forty-year-old married man. But he hadn't been willing to give it up when his time ran out.

A roared hello from inside announces T-Shirt has made a guest appearance. He is a tribal guy, has no use for American civilization beyond his criminal infatuation with white bread. "I always wanted to visit the Empire State Building," he says by way of hello to me, "until I found out they'd moved King Kong's body."

The evening is measured out in brown beer bottles, labels half-peeled, lining the wall, all the walls along the Mexican coastline, I imagine, grains of sand in an hourglass. While I am talking to Rex, Don, and Frenchy about the linear nature of time, knowledge seeps in like a stain around the fringes of my inebriation: the blonde has arrived and is up to something weird. She hasn't changed the film in her camera in at least fifty shots. When she zooms in to blind me with her flash, I see her fish hooks have tiny newspaper photos of the Willoughbys on one side, and little photos of Carole and me on the other. Where the hell —

"It's the Bitching Hour," Rex observes. "That blonde over there is even worse than your wife," he continues, not recognizing that he is now insulting My Imaginary Mistress as well. "Stay the fuck away from her."

"What do you mean?"

"Most women just steal your heart. That one will take any internal organ she can lay hands on."

"She's just a kid."

Apparently apropos of nothing, he continues. "There are a lot of Filipino nurses in the West now."

"Yeah, I know. A lot of them work like crazy, sixty or seventy hours a week, and send the money back home or save it to bring their families here."

"Well, I hear some of them are earning extra on the side. They pretend to be prostitutes to lure these married men up to their rooms—"

"Rex —"

"Hear me out. They lure these guys upstairs and then they drug them and steal one of their kidneys for black-market transplant money."

"They steal — Rex, kidneys aren't kept in zipper compartments. You're talking about major surgery. Trust me, these guys would notice when they woke up."

"That's why they always pick married men, see? Married men can't complain. If it's too scary for you, you don't have to believe it." He finishes with a flourish that makes me want to punch him in the nose.

"The only thing scary about this is that another nurse, threatened by cheap labor, would pass on the rumor." I have visions of ovens, whiff a faint trace of zyklon-B in the summer air. Make the Stranger freakish; make the Freak evil. This is precisely what happened during Willoughby's trial, as I know from a letter written by one of the jurors. She was dismissed from the trial just before closing arguments because of a family emergency. When she heard the verdict, she was so horrified by what seemed an obvious miscarriage of justice that she wrote Judge Howe to reveal a variety of what she perceived to be jury improprieties. One of the things she reported was that the jurors, like the news media, often seemed transfixed by Yesenia's transsexuality to the exclusion of all else.

I am going to lecture Rex on how easy it is to imagine the worst about someone just a little foreign to us, but instead I find myself asking, "What does this have to do with — that blonde girl?"

"I can't tell you."

"Sometimes I like to imagine taking Rex marlin fishing with a thirty-pound testline tied to his dick," Don grunts when I tell him about Rex's advice. Don and I have developed superficial and reasonably comfortable mutual impressions, yet have not entirely lost a certain wariness that goes with wondering what the wives have told each other, unfairly selected and thoroughly slanted, and not at all representative of our true characters, which was then in turn further misinterpreted by the other wife for her friend's benefit. That reduction of the self is all others know of us.

Siegel

Chapter 7: Themes

Dan's relationship with his mother-in-law was of Greek proportions. Thera Huish, Trish's mother, hated Willoughby from the moment she met him. The very ringing of the long-distance telephone call tolling her daughter's murder echoed his name, and she was instantly, clairvoyantly convinced Dan was the killer. Before any of the details of Trish's death filtered back up to Phoenix, Thera informed her family of this fact. Within a few days of Trish's death, Kay Lines, an investigator from the AG's office who was an acquaintance from her Stake in the Church of the Latter-Day Saints, became her first disciple. Lines, a big man, heavy set, oval-faced with a hairline receding above wire-rimmed glasses, pursued Dan Willoughby with a single-mindedness that made him Thera's avenging angel.

Immediately following Trish's death, the bottom seemed to fall out of Dan's life. While in Mexico arranging for his wife's body to be returned to the United States, he behaved with a stoicism so marked that the prosecution later enlisted a number of witnesses such as Dr. Lowry to testify that Dan seemed completely unemotional about her death. Under Mexican legal procedure, the Federales immediately placed Dan and his children in jail, holding them for questioning. In the two days just after the murder, Dan was assisted by an interpreter, Tomas

Arenas, and by Judge Luz Quintero Rodriquez, in filing his evidentiary statement and getting his family and his wife's body back to the United States. The judge herself sometimes drove Willoughby from consulate to courthouse, and once to her own house, appearing to be thoughtfully friendly and concerned for his children, who were always present. Tomas, a Spanish-speaking Basque who was dating the Judge, applauded Dan's stoicism for the children's sake. "If you were Mexican," he said, "there would be nothing but hysterics. We'd have to call the medics to administer oxygen and tranquillizers." Dan was horrified to learn several months later that, after being visited by the American investigators, the judge filed a new report stating Dan had tried to flirt with her. Dan believes that she did so to counter any embarrassing inference that she might have abetted a wife-murdering Lothario. Arenas, who Dan says would have corroborated his story, either was never interviewed by the state's investigators, or all trace of his interview, which should have been turned over to the defense, was inexplicably lost.

It wasn't until he had arrived back in Arizona, where he expected to be able to share his grief with Trish's family, that Dan says he allowed himself to feel the full impact of what had happened. But this too worked against him. Jamie Tepp recalls his first attempt to enter their circle of grief at the Chandler home. Dan approached Thera with outstretched arms and grief in his face — and Thera simply walked away from him. She did not confront him or ask for an explanation. She had already decided he was guilty of a murder no one else had even accused him of.

In retrospect, Dan believes Thera was setting him up from the beginning. She insisted that she, not he, conduct Trish's funeral. She made certain that her family noted Dan was not wearing his wedding ring as Trish's body lay in state — ignoring the obvious reason: Trish's wedding ring had been stolen by Yesenia, and Dan had placed his own on her finger. Thera finally did approach Dan about the events in Mexico — asking him to give a tape-recorded statement to her in the back room of her house on the very day of Trish's funeral. Her husband Sterling brought in a tape recorder, which she had him check twice to insure the recording would be a good one. According to Dan, this "debriefing" lasted some time, because he twice broke down in tears and Sterling had to shut off the recorder to allow Dan to compose himself. As bizarre as this session seemed to him, Dan hoped telling Thera as much as he knew about her daughter's death would finally convince her to set her suspicions aside and allow the grieving process to run its course.

Had he recognized the extent of Thera's enmity, he would have realized this could never happen. Thera already had contacted Kay Lines about her "feelings," and she no doubt made this recording for Lines, in an attempt to catch Willoughby in a contradiction when Lines later questioned him. But there were no contradictions, because, Dan says, he was telling the truth. Instead, the tape simply disappeared.

Thera admits to making the tape, but says she never gave it to Lines and has no idea what happened to it. When asked why she had not given the tape to the police before it became lost, she said that it had never worked, that Sterling had botched the recording job. When Thera was later cross-examined about her insistence that Dan never showed any emotion at his wife's death, she denied that he had cried at this interview. "He was sweating a lot, that's all," she insisted.

Whether Dan's emotional displays following Trish's death should even be admissible in trial is questionable, because the reasons for public displays of feelings are so complex. For example, because of crowded conditions in the court room, the Huishes ended up sitting next to me at the post-trial hearing where Yesenia's videotaped confession was first publicly aired. Because I'd already read the transcript of this confession and knew it contained an extremely graphic description of Trish's brutal murder, I was concerned that they be forewarned of what they were about to see and spoke to one of their group about it. My warning was pointless. There wasn't a horrified expression in the group, much less a tear shed, and when the court recessed following the tape, they were immediately joking and laughing with each other in the hall. No doubt the Huish family has an explanation for this, but, as I passed them in the hall, I heard Thera hush the family, whispering, "We don't want him to get the wrong idea."

In fact, Dan claims that the Huishes themselves behaved very crudely at Trish's funeral, laughing at the funeral home view, telling him to hurry when he was greeting guests come to pay their respects because they had better things to do and all this was taking far too long.

Whether or not these cross-accusations are true, my point is that, as unflattering as this behavior is, it is not all that unusual for mourners who are deeply affected to display peculiar emotions. The same confusion reigned when my younger sister died of cancer at the age of thirty-eight. You'd think it would have been different, because I knew she was going to die. I'd flown in from Arizona, and had a return ticket I kept telling myself I could always cancel. Her exploding husk twisted on the hospital bed and she turned her unrecognizable, green-tubed moon face in my direction and croaked a few incomprehensible words. I bent over the bed, and she clenched my hand and repeated the sounds, searching my eyes for signs of understanding. She'd been the beautiful and talented one, and had sometimes treated me as her "brain," that is, she often looked to me for explanations on the rare occasions she cared about them, and I thought, Maybe she's asking me to explain something now, to explain what's happening to her. This scared the shit out of me. But I leaned in again, and she wheezed into my ear a third time, and again it was incomprehensible, either from its source, or in its passage through the tubes, or simply because I could not attune my own hearing in time.

So I tried to fake it. I nodded. I smiled sternly, and blinked to show it was tough on me too, and I watched her die.

I made a complete botch of the funeral, stood up to speak and then was unable to say anything. As soon as I could, I escaped the other mourners sitting shiva at our house and crept up to the old attic where our memorabilia shared a narrow, A-framed room we had called our Library. Near the single window at the far end, beyond the paperbacks and tattered encyclopedia, hung an ancient newspaper photo of my sister winning some tennis tournament. I picked the frame off its nail and stared at the child it had failed to capture. She was no more than a brown and tan blotch with big white teeth and a pageboy haircut. Sunlight had faded the wall badly too, but the spot where the picture had been was a bright, robin's-egg blue, as it had been when we were kids together, and I stared at the spot for a long time, because it reminded me more of my sister than the picture did.

Death is so much beyond the scope of our daily focus that, when we are actually confronted by it, we are likely to do anything. While there is no specific rule of evidence forbidding it, a lawyer ought to argue that testimony concerning "peculiar" behavior at a loved one's death is more prejudicial than probative in a murder trial.

The real question is, what was Dan thinking in the weeks following the murder? Even if totally innocent, he might have suspected Yesenia's involvement, having seen her in Rocky Point on the fatal day. Was he simply too embarrassed to ask her if she had done it? Or too horrified, because Yesenia's involvement meant that he and his affair actually had set the whole thing in motion? Dan himself claims that, until police confirmed her bloody fingerprints in the Las Conchas beach house, he believed Trish had been the victim of a mistaken drug hit, as the local police had first suggested to him. (After all, who could ever find the right house around there?)

Yesenia told Lines that she spoke to Dan on the day of the funeral, but that he never even mentioned his wife's death to her. Surely this is too bizarre to accept:

"Hey, how have you been, Danny?"

"Uh, OK."

"How was the vacation?"

"OK."

"What are you doing this afternoon."

"Uh, tying up a few loose ends. Want to get together for lunch?"

Alternately, who can believe that Dan and Yesenia planned this complex and brutal murder with enough sophistication to pull it off despite everyone's vacillating museum schedule, and then failed to attend to any of the obvious details after its commission, giving a recorded statement to their main adversary while making lunch plans that were bound to raise eyebrows?

Behaving peculiarly does not make someone a murderer. Complication is not implication. For instance, Thera's actions during this time are no clearer. She denied in a sworn statement made the following year that she had ever been to Rocky Point, yet Mexican police documents (withheld from Willoughby until after his trial) indicate she was in Rocky Point only three or four days after the murder, giving a sworn statement to the Mexican police. She has denied repeatedly being involved in the American investigation as well, refuting documented meetings with Lines and Mitchell as concerning only "personal matters" unrelated to the investigation — matters which apparently prompted her to provide both men with free Matol products throughout the investigation and trial. Thera's story leaves unexplained the intensity with which Arizona authorities were pursuing Dan and Yesenia as Trish's murderers even before there was a shred of physical evidence suggesting the involvement of either. While the husband is always a suspect in his wife's murder, no American ever had been prosecuted here for a murder committed outside the United States — until the Willoughby case.

It is pointless to argue that all this "looks suspicious." The real question is, where did this enmity begin?

According to Dan, Thera Huish had hoped to progenerate a classic Mormon family, but those typically strong ties had become instruments of strangulation in her overanxious grasp. The biological father of two of her five children (Trish and Val) was killed in a plane crash when all were quite young, and she soon remarried Sterling Huish, a generally quiet and self-effacing Air Force officer with whom she had three more sons. Sterling is short and amiable, Thera tallish and thin. She looks stark in salmon. Dan describes hers as a marriage of convenience between Elvira and Lassie. According to him, Thera and Sterling never kissed, hugged, or held hands, and avoided being alone together whenever possible. Sterling provided Thera security and little argument, but his lack of interest even in adopting Trish left her feeling somewhat fatherless. Trish's brothers had trouble with their own marriages throughout the years, no doubt providing psychologists something to stroke their chins about. Although Sterling remained married to Thera, he was hardly faithful, and eventually was excommunicated from the Mormon church because of his flagrant affairs. Thera's younger son, Richard, struggled with substance abuse and died at thirty-two.

The lesson of her brothers' botched escapes wasn't lost on Trish. She was a popular child who did well in school, but beneath her submissiveness she was deeply discontented. In 1970, while still a teenager, Trish abandoned her parental home and headed for California, hoping she hadn't missed the Sixties entirely. She hadn't. Blonde with bluish-green eyes, a long-legged five-foot eight, she dove head-first into hippiedom. After a disastrous first marriage that lasted less than two years, she moved into a Bay area apartment with a female roommate who occasionally dated a guy named Dan Willoughby.

Born in a small Illinois town in 1939 and moved in his youth to Sacramento, Dan credits the moral lessons taught at home by his dad, a jeweler, and his school teacher mom as the basis for his lifelong beliefs. During the war, his father turned his jeweler's skills to manufacturing bombsights for warplanes. After graduation from high school, like many classmates who had grown up around the defense industry, Dan decided to enlist in the military, choosing the elite Airborne Ranger Reconnaissance, precursor to the Delta Force and cousin to the Green Berets.

Dan was assigned to a Mobile Tactical Unit, specially trained for emergency deployment in crisis areas. On the night of August 12, 1961, the crisis area he was sent to oversee was the Berlin Wall. Dan sat on a knoll a hundred yards from the Brandenburg Gate, then the only authorized crossing point between East and West Berlin. With his .30-caliber machine gun and rocket launcher, he watched the barbed-wire barrier gradually replaced by a six-foot concrete wall, and wondered what to do with his 4,500 rounds of ammunition. His instructions were to stay alert — and to fire when he was given that instruction. Day by day he watched the bricks go up, closing off the East Berliners from the free world. Street by street, neighborhood by neighborhood, he watched an entire nation incarcerated. Ironically, the sadness of the sight of this imprisonment never left him.

Dan did, however, come to recognize his proficiency in languages, learning German while on his tour of duty. When his tour was over, Dan enrolled in college in California, majoring in both bacteriology and international business, with an emphasis in foreign languages.

California in the Sixties hit him with emotionally explosive force. Not only did the California university system provide one of the best educations in the country, but its sex, drugs, and rock and roll were reputedly unparalleled. Celebrities like Jane Fonda, Eldridge Cleaver, Abby Hoffman, and Joan Baez bumped into you in the cafeteria line, and some of the professors there made Timothy Leary look like a trendy wimp.

But Dan kept his focus. While he indulged, and his roommates fell by the wayside, he earned both a bachelor of science in bacteriology and a bachelor of arts in international business, and added Spanish to his already fluent German.

Graduate school was on the horizon, but first Dan decided to sell off his possessions and travel in Europe with two college buddies. They drove to New York in a '46 Plymouth and got jobs as stewards on the French cruise ship, *Le Flandre*. Arriving in Le Havre, they immediately left for Germany, where they purchased a gutted Volkswagen bus, stocked it with sleeping bags and skis, and took off on an adventure through St. Moritz, Garmisch, Berchtesgaden, Innsbruck, and Mt. Chamonix. Dan worked as a ski instructor and translator. They bathed at local spas, brushed their teeth at service stations, and lived off bread, cheese, and wine. The next summer, he traveled to Scandinavia, the French Riviera, Spain, and Portugal, stopping every place he had ever heard of. He ran with the bulls in Pamplona, attended the film festival in Cannes, visited the Louvre in Paris, the Hague, the Vatican, the canals of Venice, and the casinos in Monte Carlo. He traveled with the Basque in the Pyrenees, observed the intrigues of the Casbah in Tangier, and wandered through the gold markets of northern Italy. He toiled briefly with Sicilian peasants and the students of the Left Bank, and worked construction in Innsbruck. He worked on ships in Norway, the French Riviera, and off the coast of Portugal, and attended a few classes at the Universities of Innsbruck and Heidelberg. In Barcelona, while helping to sweep the rainbow refuse from the flower markets one morning, he witnessed an assassination attempt on Franco, and later that week saved the life of a drowning Spanish boy.

When Dan returned to the States, he enrolled in what was then called the Thunderbird Institute of Foreign Trade in Phoenix (now the American Graduate School of International Management). It was then one of only two schools in the United States that specialized in international business administration. After he earned his Masters, Dan took a job with the newly formed international division of the Bank of America in San Francisco. In 1970, he took a management position with Braniff Airlines. The pay scale was only moderate by industry standards, but the perks were tailored to Dan's thirst for adventure, allowing him to travel anywhere, at any time, often with complimentary food and hotel accommodations.

Dan was just settling into his jet-set lifestyle when a girlfriend introduced him to her new roommate, Trish. Dan claims it was love at first sight. They dated for three years, working hard and living fast. Then Dan's father was diagnosed with a fatal blood disorder, and they decided to marry.

The wedding was held in a beautiful mountainside chapel called the Highland Inn, in Carmel. It was 1975. Dan was 35 and Trish 26.

Moving into a mountaintop house in the quaint, quiet town of Brisbane, overlooking San Francisco Bay, they made the changes come fast after that. Dan focused on cleaning up his life. Trish's own form of repentance, however, drew her back to the Mormon Church. For her sake, Dan, a non-practicing Catholic, agreed to convert, assuming, like many Catholics before him, it couldn't be worse than that. He didn't know what he was getting into.

In the summer of 1976, they decided to move to Arizona to complete the transition to their new life. With the money from Dan's savings and the sale of their home in Brisbane, they bought a house just a few miles from Trish's mother, Thera.

Thera had been pressuring Trish for a reconciliation, and was able to play successfully on Trish's unconditional love. Wanting to please his new wife made the move seem more like a gallant adventure than a sacrifice to Dan. He was eminently employable, and took a job offer in Phoenix from Consolidated Freight. They were both aware that Thera's involvement in their lives would have to be monitored, but felt they would be able to keep her at arm's length while Trish reestablished a relationship with her.

Dan's career prospered. The office he had taken over for Consolidated Freight went from zero profitability to netting $150,000 a month in the four years Dan worked there. The effort earned him the Manager of the Year Award, a prize that included an all-expense-paid trip to Paris for him and Trish. Approached by the Chairman of

Burlington Northern Air Freight with an offer he couldn't refuse, Dan become a district manager for them — with the side bet that, if Dan could double their profits in less than two years, BNAF would come up with a similar Parisian bonus. Dan won his bet, and became Manager of the Year for BNAF in 1983. In the process, he became personal friends with company Chairman Larry Rodberg, often visiting Rodberg's Newport Beach house with Trish.

In 1985, when Rodberg moved on to Air Express International, the largest American-owned international forwarder, Dan went with him. As a Director, Dan was able to use his German and Spanish skills dealing with overseas contacts even while he helped set up new offices for AEI in the central and western United States. He developed a reputation as a fair boss, someone you would be glad to work for, who would treat you well if you did your job. He was a thorough and meticulous person, both at work and at home. By 1990, the profits from these areas controlled by Dan were over $2 million a year, more than was coming out of districts like Los Angeles, Chicago, and New York.

In the meantime, Trish and Dan had become inescapably involved with the Huishes' marital problems. Thera humiliated Sterling on a daily basis, particularly after his extra-marital affairs became public knowledge. One night, terrified of the retribution Thera had threatened to exact, Sterling brought all his knives, guns, and ammunition to Dan's house. Dan promised to keep them out of Thera's hands, and gave Sterling cash to hide out in a hotel room for a while.

From 1980, Trish attended church regularly, and spent an increasing amount of time with her mother, seeming to have transformed herself back into the perfect daughter. She even named her own first born Thera. The product of fertility injections, Thera Willoughby was the only biological child Dan and Trish ever produced.

Because both wanted a larger family, a few years later, in 1984, they adopted Hayden, bringing him home from the hospital when he was just three days old. Dan had paid the birth mother not to have an abortion, and paid her medical bills as well. Dan is still sentimental about Hayden being the only son he will ever have to carry on his family name. How Hayden ultimately feels about it, only time will tell.

Uneasy about his commitment to the Church of the Latter-Day Saints, Dan nevertheless continued to try to please Trish — and personally "rebaptized" Sterling Huish when he was allowed to rejoin following his penitence. But Dan's personality was better suited to a Catholicism that forgave — even expected — occasional lapses to a strict regimen forbidding all alcohol and coffee — not to mention adultery. Gradually Dan drifted away from the Church of the Later Day Saints. The consequences in his case were appropriately biblical.

Thera was only too anxious to accept Trish's reconversion to the good Mormon and dutiful daughter. The two began to spend more and more time together, Trish and Dan less and less. When, in 1987, mother and daughter started a joint business venture, the mission became a focus of all their energies. Their efforts to get the fledgling enterprise off the ground seemed to require them to spend every moment, from morning to night, together in "the Nest." Trish and Dan's house became that business headquarters, so that, when Dan woke up in the morning, he found Trish and Thera already talking product. When he returned at night, he would kiss Trish in greeting, despite Thera's obvious irritation at the intrusion, and then take over care of the children. To keep Trish happy, Dan agreed that, if Trish's business began to gross $30,000/month, with Trish's share of the profits at $10,000/month, Dan would quit his job to be with her and the children. He knew this was a possibility, but he had not imagined that, as soon as 1990, he'd have to make good on his gallantry.

T&T Enterprises was a multi-level business, similar in structure to Amway, selling a liquid vitamin supplement called Matol. Much of the time the women needed to be out of the house, selling the product or training others to sell it. In 1989, the two women hired Jamie Tepp to do their secretarial work and deal with distributors who were calling the house, as well as care for the children. Hayden, the youngest son, wasn't in kindergarten yet.

Jamie had been a legal collector, had worked for a travel agency and for the Convention Bureau of Phoenix, and, in the late 1980s, found herself working for a commercial developer who took exception to her campaigning against some of their zoning interests in her time off. Answering a newspaper ad for T&T, she interviewed with Thera and Trish. Trish had a gift for making people relax and for making them feel good about themselves, and Jamie always felt her relationship with Trish was extremely personal. Because of Trish, Jamie took the job and performed it zealously.

On the day of Trish's funeral, Thera asked each of the twenty mourners gathered in her house to talk about what had been most special in their relationships with Trish. The first thing that came to Jamie's mind was that Trish had taught her unconditional love. "There was never a moment in that woman's life where she ever judged anybody." But as Jamie worked with Trish and Thera, she came to realize that Thera was the opposite of her daughter, an extremely judgmental person who was good at masking her thoughts. "Everybody loved Thera either until they got to know her, because now and then she'd let down her guard and you'd see the other side of Thera, or until they disagreed with her and she turned on them. There was such a contrast between the two of them. And Trish accepted that too, accepted the way her mom was, even though that's not the way she was herself, never handling people or controlling them or talking behind their backs when they left the office."

An addiction is something you desire before you do it and regret afterwards. A work habit is the opposite. Presumably slated to become part of T&T Enterprises himself, Dan yet had hoped that his partial "retirement" would not only free Trish to work, but allow her to pursue many of the passions she had neglected, such as singing and piano lessons and acting in amateur theater. By this time, however, Thera and Trish were extremely close in both their public and private lives, as if they couldn't exist outside each other's presence, and none of the benefits Dan had envisioned accrued. When the women traveled, they might take Dan and Sterling Huish with — but all of them would share a single hotel room. Thera saw to it that Dan and Trish were rarely allowed to travel together alone. When Dan complained to Trish, she refused to criticize her mother, perhaps feeling a need to pacify the older woman. Only when their marriage began to break down, and Dan's affair with Yesenia came out into the open, did Trish realize that she would have to choose between her mother and her husband. According to Dan, Trish started to assert her independence from both of them. In 1990, she began pursuing her own interests for the first time since she had run away.

This is essentially the biography that Dan provided me during one of our early exchanges. I confirmed much, though not all of it from school and work records.

Dan was evaluated by two different psychologists during the course of his case. The first, a Dr. Nelson, supposed that Dan has a "paranoic, anti-social personality disorder," although he admitted this diagnosis was speculative considering the testing results he obtained. This was the report submitted to Judge Howe just before Howe sentenced Dan to death.

Dr. Tatro, a psychologist later hired by Dan's appellate lawyers, obtained very similar test results when he examined Dan, but scoffed at Nelson's conclusions as completely unsupported by the data. "Not to mention," Tatro observed, "that Nelson reached his conclusions because he found Dan to be suspicious and defensive. Well, how the hell would he be when he's just been convicted of a murder he says he didn't commit and is awaiting sentencing that may condemn him to death?"

Unlike many partisan expert witnesses I've run across at trial, Dr. Tatro made no attempt to whitewash his client. Rather, he provided a perspective crucial to understanding forensic psychology, which can be used to make the most mundane character trait appear pathological. Dan's basic defense mechanism is "massive repression; his predominant characteristic is a hysterical/histrionic need to put everything in a positive light," Tatro confirmed. "But another way to characterize this behavior is that he's a positive thinker. He chooses to look at the good rather than the bad. He's an optimist." For instance, Dan volunteered early on in his conversations with Tatro, as he had with me, that he had had a nearly perfect childhood. Only later did he reveal that his mother had slit her wrists and that, when he was only twelve, she briefly sought treatment at an institution for her depression. (But it's tempting to second-guess the second-guessers. Dan did have a happy childhood, his mother's depression was relatively short-lived, and that she went on to live a long and productive life. Isn't Tatro taking a particular incident out of context and blowing it out of proportion because it is forensically delectable?)

Dan also had failed to tell me that he'd been arrested for credit card fraud in 1971. He and a bunch of buddies had charged up a fair amount of recreation on phony cards "for a lark"; Dan pled guilty to a reduced charge, and this record was later "expunged," that is, it was technically erased from his file after he'd successfully completed a probationary period.

Judge Howe told Dr. Tatro he'd primarily been interested in Dan's psychological profile before imposing the death sentence because he was unable to get a balanced sense of the man from the witnesses who had paraded through his courtroom. "Some of them characterized Willoughby as the devil. The others all said he was a saint. There was just no in-between according to these people, and before I condemn someone to death, I want to know, is there a man in here with wings?"

To Tatro, none of this came as a surprise. His evaluation of Dan showed a personality with a marked duality. "He wants to be a genuinely good man but he is capable of deviant behavior." A man with Dan's repressive personality is unaware of any bad motives and faults he has. He is likely to be manipulative. "But this is not necessarily sinister. It doesn't make him capable of murder," Tatro explained. "It makes him a salesman, an upbeat kind of guy," the kind of guy Dan's friends know him, in fact, to be. Tatro also emphasized certain compulsive tendencies, "learned early in life from a strict father, who also instilled in Dan the notion that `boys will be boys.'" Dan believes you should work hard and do the right thing — but also that it's OK to cut yourself some slack from time to time, when your work is done or you've been as good as a good man ought to be. Tatro described Dan as someone who allows himself "to take vacations from responsibility." This is likely to result in occasional binge drinking — or the kind of credit card fraud conviction Dan described. He may be an otherwise good husband and father who has affairs.

You can see the prosecutor's final question coming from a mile away: "Wouldn't murdering your wife be the ultimate vacation?"

"Historically," Tatro replied, "this would be very uncharacteristic behavior."

It makes more sense to me to try to understand Dan as I would any man I met in the normal course of my cynical and suspicious life. And I try to perceive Dan and Trish's mixed marriage through the lenses of my own, however different we may be.

"Sure you are," Rex would snort, squinting at My Imaginary Mistress across the room as if she had a bull's-eye tattooed on her rump. "What 'happily' married middle-aged man hasn't imagined his wife dead and himself with a million bucks and a fuck-monster girlfriend, returning to the adventurous wanderings of his youth?"

"I thought you were afraid she'd steal your kidney if she got you alone?"

"What guy's dick hasn't said to him, 'So who needs two kidneys?'"

When we happily married men walk up that flight of stairs behind hypnotic Philippino hips, each of us knows what he will lose. We only ask to be allowed to pretend otherwise.

Chapter 8: Lying to Ourselves

In the morning when I arise, I am pretty sure Carole is only pretending to be asleep. I'm vaguely aware that she has been up prowling part of the night, probably cleaning up not only this bedroom but the kitchen as well, perhaps reading a magazine article. If she is lying here now waiting for me to do something for her that-I-would-know-if-I'd-been-paying-attention-all-these-years, I am about to flunk another of her tests. I'm willing to try, but, like a student who has relied on the text when he should have been paying attention in class, I don't understand how her questions relate to my knowledge. Only the pounding in my head seems completely real, so, like the student, I close my book and head for the student union.

Actually, I sneak out to the kitchen, pretending I don't want to wake her up from her pretend sleep. Everyone else is up and gone already, so, I try working. But it is not the book I'm supposed to be writing. It is what I have imagined in continuation of the previous evening, after everyone went to sleep and I slept-walked back out into another version of the living room, and found My Imaginary Mistress waiting:

There was a table lamp on next to the couch. When she looked up, her nakedness stretched from her long neck, down her throat, and went on through the couch and floor, into the sand and earth below, much further than my old, weak eyes could follow. "You can change everything in a second, just by deciding," she told me.

"Deciding what?" Pretending not to know was merely the first line of defense that occurred to me.

I sighed, and ached. And hear Don's jeep coming up the drive, before I can figure out how not to make a jerk of myself even in my own imagination.

Closing my laptop, I wander out the back door to help unload groceries or make drinks, only to find they have already gone around the front. Is it T-Shirt or Hemingway whose scornful laughter echoes down the rocks, among the waves?

Happily, it is T-Shirt. His laugh is cosmic, Chaucerian, world-embracing, not bitter or scornful, as I imagine the writer's would have been. He is sporting a black tank-top with the lettering and crest they apparently use at Vassar these days.

"Professor!" he shouts, waving a beer bottle at me.

"Mr. Shirt," I respond happily, before poking my head into the refrigerator and discovering he has grabbed the last beer. "What are you up to?"

"Stopped by on my vending machine rounds. Little devils fill up faster than a skinny man's bladder on a warm night. And you?"

"Just looking forward to another day of being led around by my nose."

Bev and Don have already unpacked, not groceries, but scuba tanks. "Rex has beaten us into submission," Bev sighs. "We're going diving with him despite the rough water."

"It seemed like a good compromise," Don adds. "We'll have to keep it short because of the Commodore's Ball tonight."

"Five minutes would be good," Bev snorts. "We'll be puking our guts over the side of the boat before we even get out there. Want to come?"

"Ah, maybe next time." I ask about a restaurant named Manny's and a gay bar I think is called Arturo's, where Yesenia used to hang out. Of course, T-Shirt knows the latter place better. "I'm on my way to do the machines in that direction anyway. Can take you right now."

"Is it safe?" I ask.

T-Shirt tosses me something and roars with laughter. It's a condom from one of his vending machines. "That'll make it safer than hanging around here waiting for your wife to wake up."

On the way over there, I tell T-Shirt the prosecution's embellishment of the meeting between Willoughby and the Patinos, Yesenia and her brother Tony, that took place at Manny's.

Explaining Yesenia's presence in Rocky Point the morning of the murder is a sticking point for me. Dan claims that she knew about the family's trip from conversation back in November, when he booked the bungalow. In a lame-ass attempt to prove he was serious about reconciling with his wife, he took Yesenia to Las Conchas to check out the area where he planned to rent for the February Family Outing. The trip was to assure himself the area was appropriate for his children, and, as I discovered years later, it's difficult to find a particular house in Las Conchas, so a guide is helpful. According to Dan, his sexual relations with Yesenia had ended months earlier, when he had reconciled with Trish, yet Yesenia continued to rely on him for financial support and refused to give up hope of having Dan for herself. Hoping to part amicably, Dan had encouraged her to reconcile with her ex-husband, Jack Mielke, whom Yesenia had continued to see sporadically for years, at least in part because of their "adopted" son, who usually stayed with Jack. Jack, then living in Oregon, was less than enthusiastic (she was, after all, loco), but drove down to Chandler in October with a trailer to pick up some of Yesenia's possessions. Dan hoped he'd be back soon, before too many more rent checks came due.

Yesenia and Tony already had friends (and perhaps drug connections) in Rocky Point, and obviously knew the town better than Dan, who was only going there for the first time because Trish's brother had raved about it. So three months later, Yesenia might have gone to Las Conchas on her own initiative, stalking either Trish or Dan, or both, without Dan's knowledge. Then, the morning of Trish's murder, Dan accidentally ran into Yesenia and Tony, on the beach next to Manny's Bar. Dan claims it was a chance encounter, when he came into town to rent ATVs for the kids to race on the sand. The prosecution alleged, on the other hand, and Yesenia testified, at least in one of her versions of events, that she and Dan spent the morning at Manny's confirming the details of the murder they had planned back in Arizona. The prosecution's story goes something like this:

They'd been waiting on the beach for some time before Tony saw Willoughby walking along the sand in Levi jacket and pants. Tony had been worrying about this moment ever since his sister's boyfriend bought him the pick-up, but he couldn't very well have refused to drive her down here to meet him.

Yesenia was so busy hiding behind her dark glasses and pretending to be mysterious, she didn't see the guy until he practically sat down on top of them. Willoughby asked her if she'd made it OK, and she jumped up and gave him a big nasty kiss, lots of tongue. Tony wondered if Willoughby knew about her previous life as Alberto. Well, it was none of his business.

Dan gestured up the beach, to where the bay curved around and you could barely make out a nest of new development. He pointed to his watch, and Yesenia covered it playfully with one hand. The three of them walked up the beach into the restaurant part of Manny's, so they wouldn't be so conspicuous, talking out in the open. Tony ordered a Corona and some shrimp soup, and tried to stay out of the discussion. As far as he was concerned, this was just about money.

"We gotta talk about it, Danny," Yesenia told him.

"I'm goin' to the Hombre's," Tony informed them, getting up from the table. He didn't like the sound of it.

As Tony got up to go to the can, Willoughby started talking to her in a low voice, in English. He liked talking to her in Spanish, but there was less chance of anyone at the Mexican cafe understanding what they might overhear if he spoke in English.

When Tony got back from taking a leak, Yesenia told him they were going to drop Willoughby back where he'd parked his Blazer.

"We got time to finish lunch?" Tony asked.

"We got to stake the place out," Yesenia told him under her breath, doing her spy thing again. "Besides, you don' wanna do somethin' like this on a full stomach," she informed him, like she knew from years of experience. "It's all coming down in a few hours."

Coming down or going down? What was the right way to say it, he wondered?

The prosecution's version is more saleable than Willoughby's claim of a completely coincidental meeting. As Rex indelicately puts it in dismissing Dan's story about the November trip to the bungalow, "What kind of a jerk-off whips out his dick to show one woman what he plans to do with another?" If I were asked to imagine a third explanation for events, based on my own (and Rex's) understanding of human nature, I'd make up one evolving out of Dan and Yesenia's unresolved demands of each other.

As the psychologist, Dr. Tatro, explained, Dan is the kind of person who wants to be everything to everyone, who wants to please everyone. He not only wanted both Yesenia and Trish, but he wanted them both to be happy. So he told them both he loved them, gave them both more or less concrete reassurances. Sometimes you can only give people honest reassurance by lying to yourself, so it's entirely possible Dan never even confronted in his own mind all the aspects of his affair with Yesenia. (Too, when the State is threatening to use anything you say against you so that it can put you to death, explaining *anything* is probably a bad idea.) In any event, Dan may have promised himself in November, when he was with Trish, that he was breaking things off with Yesenia, but when he was with Yesenia he really couldn't quite imagine how to do that. In taking Yesenia to look at the beach house, Dan was demonstrating to himself that he had two women, reveling in his own sexuality at the same time he was expressing his confusion over it.

So what, after all, what the hell did he say when he took Yesenia down to Rocky Point and showed her the beach house? According to Yesenia, it was something like:

"Nice, huh?"

"Let's go in and make love," she'd said, squeezing his arm in the stiff breeze. The breeze wasn't all that was stiff. But the doors were locked.

"When are you going to rent it and bring me here for the weekend?"

"Maybe after I bring my family."

"What?"

"I'm going to bring my family here first. But we'll come, another time."

"But Dan —- No! I want you to take me there, now!"

"I'm sorry, Chiquita, but my family —"

"I want to be your family, Danny! Don't you see? The kids, they love me too. We get along great. All you have to do is divorce Trish —"

"Now, Yesenia —"

"I won't stand for it, Danny. Get rid of her!"

Maybe he never actually said to Yesenia, "I'm breaking it off, that's it." Or if he did, he made love to her "one last time," and then reneged. After all, he kept paying her bills, even after the murder. Bottom line: even if he was waiting for one of the two women in his life to leave him, because he couldn't stand to make that decision himself, this screwed-up episode is not all that incredible. The same would be true for the psychology of the women. Trish didn't want to leave, perhaps because she didn't know he had continued to deceive her. Yesenia didn't, because she liked to imagine she was irresistible to men and could always have her way.

But Yesenia would have seen, when she heard about the family vacation, that Dan and Trish were not to be separated as easily as she had hoped. Maybe Dan used the cop-out that Trish couldn't stand the thought of divorce for religious reasons. So Yesenia had months to brood and plan. She'd had a confrontation with Trish in Chandler, and promised herself that she'd get even with the imperious Mrs. Willoughby. When she came back to Rocky Point on her own, to get her drugs, she had her connection, El Negro, take her back out to the vacation house in Las Conchas. *They stood in the dark, the surf pounding behind them, Yesenia staring and staring at the rental house, El Negro thinking, Is she going down on me or what? She paid for her drugs, most of the time, with the money she got from that fool gringo, but this was extra, he'd only agreed to show her how to get out to this place because he thought, hey, a moonlit beach, a hot piece... .*

"Can you get me a piece?" she asked suddenly.

"Hey what?"

"A gun. Can you get me a gun?"

"Sure. What kind?"

"It's for ... personal protection. Small. Cheap. I only need to protect myself maybe once."

"You got fifty American?"

"And a silencer."

El Negro frowned, darkness upon darkness upon darkness. "Silencers are not so easy."

"But you can do it, can't you? You can get anything." She shrank against him, not even pretending it was the chill of the breeze.

Let's see if I can get you first, he thought.

But he never did come up with the silencer, and Yesenia gave up that idea. She was a person with more ideas than resources, and the latter, except for Dan, tended to be erratic at best. *One afternoon, she was consoling herself in the Capri bar on Van Buren, then the heart of Phoenix's "tenderloin" district, flirting with the bartender, when she happened to notice one of the wall decorations was a steel ball hanging on a chain. She thought it was "cute."*

"Can I have that?" she asked, vaguely intrigued by the object, and always interested to see what she could get out of a man with her charms.

"Honey, you can have anything you want."

She paid for the murder weapon with a kiss.

According to the police, on the February day he was leaving for Rocky Point with HIS FAMILY, Dan came by to mollify her, and she hit him up good.

"Five hundred bucks? I'll only be gone a couple days."

"I have to entertain myself while you're off having fun with your FAMILY, don't I? You want me to stay out of trouble, don't you?"

"But five hundred! What are you going to do with it?"

"Never mind. You just go have fun with your FAMILY... ."

In the end he gave it to her, but it gnawed at him, not just the amount, which wasn't as easy to come by as it once had been, but what she planned to do with it. He hoped she'd go on a shopping spree at Victoria's Secrets or take a bus to visit Mielke. But he was pretty sure she was going to buy drugs, and he was pretty sure she bought them ... down in Rocky Point.

I imagine that the more he thought about it, the more he worried. He'd begged her not to do coke around him, and knew she'd only pretended to quit. She could really fuck herself up with five hundred American, get into a shitload of trouble. So the morning he arrived in Rocky Point, Dan found himself making an excuse to go into town to check out available activities, and instead making a beeline for Manny's, their favorite bar. You could get anything from her friends at Manny's, she'd told him. That's probably where she went to get her drugs. That's where he'd find her if she'd come here to make trouble.

According to Dan, Yesenia never had to ask him directly for the money, but simply took it out of the utilities and rent account he had set up for her at Thunderbird Bank. Likewise, Dan denies going to Manny's to see her but guesses she knew he would get there eventually if she waited around long enough. In any event:

Yesenia and Dan "accidentally" found each other at Manny's the morning of the murder, because the lovers knew each other well enough to know the other might be there. Having confirmed his worst fear, though, that she'd taken his money and come down here to buy drugs with it, Dan didn't know what to do with her. He told her his family was waiting back at the beach house, that he had just come by to make sure she was OK.

"I want to have a drink with you," she said.

"Manny's isn't serving. It's some kind of holiday. I just don't have the time."

"I want to have a drink with you, Danny," she whined, pressing his arm against her body. "We can go somewhere else. Vina del Mar, they got wine and beer."

"I can't, Chiquita —"

But she pled with him with such intensity that he finally agreed to have just one, and followed her and Tony in his pick-up the short distance to the other restaurant in his Blazer. Dan stuck to his guns there. What was the point of bringing his family all the way down here for a reconciliation with Trish just to abandon her for an afternoon fuck with Yesenia? And Yesenia still had the five hundred bucks, for chrissake. Or at least she said she did.

After Dan left her in the Vina del Mar, Yesenia had a second beer and thought. It was time. She was tired of waiting for Dan to make a choice. She had come down here to make something happen. She shouldered the enormous purse and told Tony she was going to the little girls' room.

In a sworn deposition given after the trial, Yesenia confessed to her part in this scenario at Manny's. Clearly it does not match the prosecution's version of what went on the morning of the murder, sold to the jury at trial with Yesenia's and Tony's testimony.

The more I look at Dan and think about his situation, the more I imagine I recognize pretty common patterns of behavior. "Is a murderer different from you and me?" I ask T-Shirt, F. Scott Fitzgerald to his Hemingway, as we get in his truck.

"Yeah," he says. "A murderer has more balls than you do."

For once I think he's wrong.

I doubt eating a bowl of shrimp soup at Manny's is going to mean much to me anyway, but maybe I will discover some obvious hole in Tony's story, such as the complete absence of toilet facilities. Maybe I will meet El Negro at Arturo's and ask him about a silencer....

Arturo's is not at all like the touristy Senor Frog's in Mazatlan where Yesenia was captured, nor is it an extended ma-and-pa cantina, like Manny's, or a Spring

Break Bar, like JJ's. Neither is there anything particularly gay about the place, in any sense I can see. It is dark, with a Formica bar and unfinished wooden chairs and tables. The black and white photos on the wall may be of Mexican drag queens or the owner's relatives, and I have enough dumb questions to ask already.

T-Shirt starts for me. "Hey, Rubio, you remember a woman named Yesenia, used to come in here sometimes. Murdered the rich gringo lady?"

"Loud maricon," Rubio nods.

I explain that Yesenia wasn't actually a transsexual, but a hermaphrodite who had had her penis cut off. Rubio looks at me with disgust, then at T-Shirt. T-Shirt roars with laughter, and claps me on the shoulder. "Well, at least she made a choice!"

I know he is talking about me, unable to choose between being a writer or a lawyer, a husband or a lover (even in fiction!), or a — Who is he to talk? But T-Shirt at least has made his choice to be none of these. And he seems happy.

Rubio has no recollection of seeing "the loud maricon" with her brother and a gringo back on a February morning several years ago. He thinks I'm crazy for even asking such a stupid question, and assures me additionally that he probably wasn't on in the morning anyway. He's only there now because the regular bartender has been arrested for breaking and entering.

I wish I had pictures of Yesenia and Tony to validate what Rubio might be able to tell me. The only ones I've seen were in the newspaper, more like shadows creating the illusion of a face. But what am I even hoping for? For someone to say, "I saw them! He did it!"? I won't believe them anyway. No, what I want is some telling detail, some little anecdote that is not exactly related to the murder, but will expose a character trait on which the swinging door of my plot can hinge more solidly.

I explain this to T-Shirt, who rubs his stomach thoughtfully. "Agustin can get you a picture. He will if Frenchy asks him. Frenchy eats his fried chicken," he adds ambiguously.

We load his bag of coins and cases of condoms and cologne back into his pick-up.

"I can't face the question of when to go back to the States," I confide in T-Shirt on the way back to Bev and Don's.

"You going back to the States or what?" he asks me in an artificial voice. "That help?"

"What'll I do if I go back?"

"Change your name to T-Shirt Mack. I'll sell you the franchise cheap. What are you going back for? You miss TV?"

"There's a new **X-Files** on this weekend," I shrug. "Scully and Mulder investigate the inability of the Cubs to win a pennant. And if that's not enough, I can go to their HomePage on the Web and talk to a bunch of other people with no lives." T-Shirt is unconvinced, so I ask him to stop for a case of beer.

"What kind?"

"Let's see what they have."

"No way, gringo," he laughs. "It's not like that here. There's a Tecate store. There's a Corona store. There's a Dos Equis store."

"Tecate." So we go to a dirty hole in the wall on the main drag, where there are about a thousand brown bottles of Tecate half-packed, half-swimming in ice, and four or five guys that must work there stacking and unstacking crates of the beer, but when I ask for a case, they scratch their heads like they've never had such a crazy request before. T-Shirt prevails, however, even gets them to open a couple bottles for us before we leave, and I pay twice. The rent on the bottles and the crate costs nearly as much as the beer itself.

As I'm carrying the case back to the pickup, I walk right into T-Shirt's ample rump. For the first time since I've known him, T-Shirt is actually frowning, at a pair of dark blue police cars parked across the street.

"What is it? A robbery?"

"Fucking Federales. If they haven't robbed somebody yet, they will."

"This got something to do with Sr. Brown's eviction of local gringos?" I guess from worried conversations I've been hearing over the past few days.

T-Shirt grunts. From the rear window of the second car, a pair of aviator sun glasses are aimed at us.

"They're still cops, right? They won't just start shooting people because Brown says so. Will they?" I set the case down in the back of the pick-up carefully, replacing my own in it so as not to break any exotic open-container laws punishable by exposure to automatic weapons fire. T-Shirt climbs into the driver's seat with his beer and fires the engine before answering.

"They'll do whatever Brown tells them to do. Sr. Brown is a fucking pillar of fucking society. The way rust is a monument to time."

"Drive slowly," I suggest. And suddenly he is roaring with laughter again.

Siegel

Chapter 9: The Commodore's Other Ball

Carole still has not returned by the time the Sunset Revelers awaken me from my nap. Bev informs me that she went into town to shop for souvenirs with Betty, the lady next door, and probably stayed for happy hour at Playa Bonita or Latitude 31. (Frenchy calls the bar Attitude 31, setting me to imagining the other thirty attitudes.)

"Still batching it?" T-Shirt asks too loudly when I squeeze out onto the veranda. "His wife ran off on him!" he laughs to Rex.

"So what?" says Rex. "We have ice."

Cocktails, which I don't need, lead to a discussion of dinner, but only a discussion. Tonight is the Commodore's Ball, and T-Shirt is expected to perform his annual barbecue and self-immolation. Queasy even before I heard about the tendency of his greasy t-shirts to burst into flame around an open fire, I yet am lured out of the house by the prospect of Rex's ham radio, which will at least allow me to create the impression that I have attempted to make contact with my responsibilities on the home planet, even if it means people named "Bear Claw" and "Three Bellies" will know all about my problem.

Rex tells me all about his own espousa's latest antics involving shampoo and a complete ignorance of — or just plain insensitivity to — the basic biochemistry of recycling. She has refused to sleep with him until he apologizes. "The old wrecking-ball-and-chain" has split for the States with all her nurse friends. Rex's post-rejection complaints of his wife's, or any woman's, activities are as regular as farts after meals, and there is more to the comparison than regularity and sequence. Not that I am in any position to criticize, but I suggest he at least may be exaggerating.

"Don't tell me YOU, of all people, think you know the difference between fantasy and reality. Mack, the problem with you is that you're afraid of having to own up to your fantasies."

"I'd have a better shot at telling the difference if I had a little hard information to go on for a change. How about that shortwave radio?"

Rex sniffs the air for a moment, frowns slightly, and turns toward his house. "Not a perfect night," he says, "but who knows."

"What kind of weather do you need for radio?"

"Who's talking about radio?" he asks blankly.

Rex's house is one enormous room with a kitchenette and a square pressed-wood workshop, with, I presume, sleeping quarters in the loft. Computer parts and what must be other useful junk are strewn all over mismatched benches, chairs, and picnic tables. He leads me to the sea-side of the bungalow, points out the picture window across a declining plain of grapefruit-sized rocks. The only thing between us and the sea is a row of wind chimes strung from a set of gallows of, I am guessing, Rex's own construction. It is as if an entire family has been executed and left in the sun and salt to dry. Some of the chimes are eight or ten inches long, and these already tinkle — or dong, because they seem to be made of cast iron — in the substantial breeze. Others, however, are enormous, several feet of cast iron, like blunderbuss barrels, and would require a wind named after an angry woman to sound. The gigantic chimes barely move under current conditions.

They represent, Rex explains, one of his experiments with music. A particular westerly wind known as El Ninos, he has theorized, will blow each of them in order and, because they are carefully weighted as well as toned, for the proper duration, to reproduce a Gregorian Chant known as The Breath of God. "I've got the octaves right, but timing and duration are a problem."

I snort my skepticism, but I am again taken aback by the man's unflagging energy in following through on his crackpot schemes. I am this nuts myself.

He's scalloped the roof and rearranged the water tanks to create wind-tunnels and back drafts.

"Has it ever worked?"

"Of course, but no one is ever around to hear it. And you could hear it all over the bay if it happened."

"Like the green flash."

"Right."

"How's the weather for radioing?"

"Who you gonna call at this hour?"

He has a point there. I suggest we do something local, like put out an All-Gringo Alert on my wife. Instead we end up with about sixty others at a dilapidated clubhouse a few sand dunes inland from Bev and Don's.

It is a cylindrical, two-story affair which looks even taller because it sits on one of the highest dunes around, like a blue-frosted wedding cake on a pedestal. Food is being served cafeteria-style on the top floor, beer on the lower level. "Easier to get at what's really essential," Rex explains. Less far to fall, I think. On the volleyball court, an Elvis impersonator, of the rotund, white-fringed leather sect, is doing the best he can considering the Mexican border guards refused to allow him to "import" his equipment for this gig when he refused to pay a tax equivalent to their net worth. (These routine bribes, Frenchy tells me, are initiated when a border guard walks up to you and says, "You got a little cream for my coffee?") Squealing groups of three or four grey-haired gringo ladies, beer foam enhancing the fur on their upper lips, periodically rush across the court at the King, once or twice accidentally knocking him to the sand.

The Commodore's Ball is an annual ritual for the local gringos. Tonight is a particularly inauspicious night for an outsider, because the sole topic of conversation seems to be the rent strike or whatever it is that Rex has organized against Sr. Brown. Interspersed among horror stories about what Brown has done to rivals in the drug trade, Rex's bravura remarks seem like so many sardines swirling mindlessly among much larger fish with sharp teeth. Every time someone asks my legal opinion about the landholders' rights, Rex interrupts my plea of ignorance with his own authoritative pronouncements. Ultimately, I find it boring to listen to someone who knows even less than I do ("Unless you're hoping to sleep with her!" I can hear Rex say), and I arrange to stagger drunkenly out of the club before ever reaching the food on the upper floor.

At first I think I might watch T-Shirt's grubby-fisted performance around the big, out-door barbecue pit twenty yards from the back of the club. I can make out the special t-shirt he is wearing for the occasion: a large hairy ball on the front, orbited by the words "Commodore's Ball," and a similar insignia on the back of the t-shirt, labeled "Commodore's Other Ball." T-Shirt's hearty "haw haw" splits the night and his belly protrudes aggressively toward the fire as he counts coup against his elemental enemy by jutting his beard into the sparks and flipping a rack of ribs. Even from my doorway I find the smoke dissuasive, and stumble away from the spectacle.

To my left, I know, is Sandy Beach, where most of the campers have pitched their tents. I have no good excuse to go there, except that it is dangerous and I might get into a fight. My drunken self, however, realizes I will lose such a fight, perhaps badly, and I am not that interested in punishing myself in this particular way. (My drunken self is quite skilled at self-appraisal, perhaps because I drink more than the people you hear about who do crazy things when drunk, or perhaps because inhibitions have nothing to do with my particular brand of cowardice.) Besides, I ought to be at home sulking when Carole pulls up, hoping to catch me having a good time without her. So I turn right and try to follow the shoreline around the little point and back to Bev and Don's, but the sandy stretches give way to outcroppings of rock as I pass beneath the threatened, ramshackle homesteads the gringos have been talking about all night. Drunk and in the dark, I fall and cut and bruise myself at least twice before I give it up and claw my way back to the dirt road and then limp to Bev's residence.

Parts of this walk are missing from memory, and I am only dimly aware of wedging myself into the little bathroom off of my bedroom and getting my pants down with the intention of addressing my damaged legs with hydrogen peroxide. The bathroom is also a good place to throw up, of course. Knowing I'm strategically positioned, I slide the door to my room nearly shut to block out its single, bare light bulb which seems itself to be dreaming, throbbing with illusions of disco. I lean back on the toilet, and close my eyes, letting things reel for a time.

I don't know for how long, except that, when I open my eyes, the reeling has stopped and my nausea subsided. The bathroom is damp and dark. My neck is killing me, and, as I roll my head carefully along the side of the porcelain toilet bowl against which it has been propped, I look out the cracked door into my bedroom, still lit by that single bulb.

The blonde girl, my IM, is naked, straight-backed in the chair next to the little dresser I have been using as a desk, her profile alert and relaxed at the same time. My first actual view of her body, strong shoulders, muscled back, with wide, small breasts, forces me to realize that I have been imagining her like this for the past several days. She is completely focused on something I can't quite make out at first, and when I do I can't quite believe it. She is leaning forward slightly in the chair now, the tips of her small breasts erect and pointed like the noses on twin hunting dogs. I watch her watch the two-inch cockroach with an inexplicable certainty that an enormous tongue is going to snap out of her mouth and snatch the roach off the wall without even disturbing the dust, without leaving even a wet spot, and that a second later there will be just the slightest tickling movement in her throat to verify what I have seen.

Her lips are full and slightly open, like animals breathing at the bottom of a sea. But she doesn't move, and neither do I, for several minutes. When she finally speaks, I start at the quiet, controlled voice, completely detached from the eyes still sighted on the huge fat bug. "When I was little, I was terrified of cockroaches. We lived in a place where there were a lot of them. You couldn't keep them out of the bathroom, the kitchen, even the bedroom. So I was freaked all the time. Not that anybody gave a damn. Except for my father. One day he got me a frog, a big green one, and I got to love it because he had given it to me. He fed it for me every day, so I didn't have to worry about that, until he suddenly went away."

She doesn't look over at me. Is there someone else in the room, soiling my bed perhaps, to whom all this is directed? Is she practicing some sort of dramatic monologue?

She breathes visibly, and the smell of sex fills the room. "The frog ate cockroaches. Someone had to feed it a dozen live roaches a day. Once I decided it had to be me, my loathing shattered like a window pane. It took no time at all to learn to catch roaches. And that changed everything. Changed my whole perspective as soon as I *wanted* the little bastards. Before I'd imagined they were everywhere, in my underpants, in every half-open drawer crawling all over the silverware, in my sandwich the second I put it down. Suddenly there didn't seem to be that many of them. The more I hunted them, the harder they became to find. I was anticipating them now, *wanting* them to be there. I was scuttling around in the corner of the yard at night, running through the house with them squirming in my hands, and I was *laughing*. I liked being the hunter. I decided from then on I'd always be the hunter."

The girl is perfectly still now, perfectly focused for a moment, and when I sense she is about to move, when there is the slightest tensing of neck muscle suggesting she is about to turn her head in my direction — I close my eyes.

When I open them, she is gone. But I have heard the chair scraping as it was pushed back. I know I have not imagined this tableau. I pry myself off the floor and crawl up and out into the little bedroom. In the darkness of the room, there is a pool of blackness on my bed, where I had imagined her audience to be, a black hole. A pool of blood? Her black t-shirt. I pick it up and turn on the table lamp next to the bed. There is no writing on it, no identification of any sort, not even a laundry tag.

And there are the papers, the notes for my murder book, neatly stacked on top of the dresser. I am not that neat.

And there is no sign of Carole. Stripping off the rest of my clothing, I flick off the light and lay down carefully. I lie awake on my bed in alcoholic urgency, wondering what I will do if my suddenly not-so-Imaginary Mistress comes back in here looking for her t-shirt, which I happen to be holding in one hand. But eventually, she does not.

There hasn't been a sound in the house for fifteen or twenty minutes.

I pace to the window and look out. There's no fire on the beach. No stars in the sky. No white Camry coming up the dirt road. Are these people fucking with me? Only the Japanese could be that considerate. Or is this just another chapter of my bizarre but essentially meaningless life? Carole is fine, I tell myself, I'm just guilty because I don't know for sure, because maybe there's something I should have done that I haven't. I lay back down, willing the night to kill itself.

Chapter 10: Apologies to Heisenberg

From bags and drawers, Bev is pulling raw materials to be hacked into lunch. I point at one long half-loaf of bread, covered at the broken end by what looks like a large balloon. "What's that?"

"Bread condom. It's one of Rex's inventions."

I check my ridicule. "Does it work?"

"Better than the dual KY Jelly and maple syrup warmer."

I am pleasantly surprised to find Carole lying next to me when I awake, still asleep, or is until, as I take my coffee to the veranda, T-Shirt shouts up from the road. "Heard your old lady made quite a scene at the Plaza last night!"

I glance surreptitiously around to determine if I can pretend he is shouting at someone else in some other, near-by house, but every one of Bev's neighbors is now leaning over their porch walls and out their windows and staring at me.

"That band must be pretty well worn out!" he shouts.

"You're wrong about Willoughby," Rex says flatly from behind me. He has a beer.

"What?" I half-whisper, half-gasp.

"About the sperm whale thing," he says, as if explaining himself.

"How's that?" I manage.

"At the party, that first night, you said Willoughby was sitting on death row waiting to get hit with enough juice to flash fry a sperm whale," he continues seriously. "But Arizona doesn't electrocute people. Up to 1990 they had gas. Now it's lethal injection, with either option for those sentenced under the old regime. Arizona used to be a hanging state," he grinned at Bev, "until some fat broad with a syphilitic neck was decapitated." He goes on to explain that electrocutions typically involve cycles of two thousand and one thousand volts, because actually insuring death without literally setting a man on fire turns out to be a pretty tricky business.

"Um," I say, calling on my near-barbecue experience with T-Shirt, "kind of like burning meat on the outside without cooking it properly on the inside."

"I'm thinking about selling an ad concept to the cotton industry," Rex confides. "Did you know that they have to dress the condemned in one hundred percent cotton because synthetics flare up?"

The man definitely hails to the beat of a different laugh track.

"Both Trish and I had made many mistakes in our lives," Dan told me, "but we knew how to resolve them between us. As we seemed to grow apart in our relationship, we both admitted `failings' and chose a course of action to get us back on the right path. We went to marriage counseling. We decided that she had to lay down the law with her mother about her wanting to spend more time with her husband and family. Trish did this and it was not accepted well by her mother."

Dan writes this from death row, where any statement that is not self-serving is a suicide note. But it is the kind of statement one might doubt had David made it about Bathsheba and her mother. "I planned a trip to Mexico for the weekend. It was the week after Valentine's Day of

1991. We could spend some quality time with the family and on the beach and in a rented house in a nice area. I bought her and my children presents, bought a lot of fireworks to light on the beach.... But all this came to an end when Trish was killed by a sick, vindictive Mexican National on February 23, 1991...."

To get some perspective on Dan's version of his family life, I asked Jamie about Trish and Dan's relationship after 1989. As the ex-Cinderella for T&T Enterprises, Trish and Thera's company, which was based in the Willoughby home, Jamie was privy to everything that went on in the extended family.

"I didn't necessarily see trouble in the marriage as much as I felt there was a separation of the family and the business that needed to happen. Trish had no life that didn't include her mother and T&T Enterprises. I would get there at 8 or 9 in the morning and her mother would be there. I would leave around 3:30 or 4 and her mother would be there. If I had to call Trish at night, Thera would pick up the phone. I'd think, they're just really getting into the business, just starting to be successful, so I wrote it off to this. This is what you do when you're trying to get a business off the ground. By the end of '89, there was a lot of traveling without the husbands, a lot of corporate stuff. By the beginning of '90, I started noticing that Danny wasn't around that much any more, and he and Trish were never together. He was taking a lot of business trips, but I remember saying to my sister, he's having an affair. I mean, leaving on a business trip on Friday night and coming back Monday morning; how much business can you do in Mexico over the weekend?

"It seemed like their life was his business, her business, and then they had children in the home together, but even that was mostly on Sundays, when they'd go to church and had a family day with the kids. In 1990, I thought they just don't spend a lot of time together. And then I thought, maybe I just think that because my husband and I are together all the time, we work the same hours, we always have evenings and usually weekends. It's changed," she said, pausing. "That's the way it used to be." I hear Jamie and Chris are divorced now, but, for all I know, this conversation with me was the first time Jamie was speculating out-loud about her own marriage.

"I used to say to Chris," she continued, talking about her husband in the past tense although I'd been introduced to him moments before, "I don't know how they do it. They're not together enough. So I think Trish knew there were problems long before she admitted it, or at least before she showed any signs of admitting it. About mid-1990, in the summer, we started having some discussions where we were ragging about our husbands, he's not doing this, he should be doing that more, and the big focus was Danny's job. Trish always believed, and I do too, that the hardest thing about working in a company like Danny did was all the politics and the pressure and not having control. Our business, T&T, wasn't like that. We decided how hard we were going to work and we could see what our efforts meant. So we used to say Danny had to get out of that `job job.' That `job job's' going to kill him. So Trish figured that we were getting into a position where Danny could quit what he'd been doing and work with us. And pretty soon after that, Danny came in real stressed because he was being pressured at work not to give bonuses to his employees, and one thing I learned about Danny since from the people he worked with was that he was real loyal to his employees. So there was a big blow-up between him and corporate, and he quit. Then I saw a real release, a lot of pressure off him and Trish.

"This was in July or August. By September, Octoberish, he started getting involved in the T&T

business, doing this and that, but it was very apparent that Trish wanted him to have his own group, not to be tied to theirs. So it would be his thing, so he wouldn't be riding on someone else's coattails. So Trish and Thera tried to act as just his distributors. But Danny wasn't ready to commit. It was the first time in thirteen years the man didn't have to work, and I thought the man was having fun playing, and of course now I know he was having fun playing around. But he seemed frustrated. He didn't have any direction. If he didn't want to do T&T, that's fine, but you've got to have some purpose. And he'd been making $75,000 a year, and now nothing, and I knew that Trish's draws weren't enough to cover that in those days.

"One of the things we talked about was credit cards. Danny would charge stuff and not tell her, and then, at the end of the month, there are all these bills to pay. I know, because I've been through that with Glen. I told her to let Danny live on his unemployment for a while, to let that be his fun money. The next thing I know, she comes in and says, Danny doesn't have any more credit cards, just American Express for emergencies and a Master Card for business. I said okay. So at the end of November, I'm planning for our Christmas party and I need Danny to pick something up down in Phoenix, so I called him and he agreed and went down there, but then he calls and says he wants to use the Master Card to pay for it. I said go ahead, it's business. He says no, I want to talk to Trish about it. I said she's busy doing something in the kitchen with her mom, but he insists I go ask her if it's OK. I'm thinking, what's the big deal? I didn't know what they had agreed to, but I told Trish, and she just laughed at how hard he was trying to do what they'd agreed. She was so proud of him, and told me to go back and tell him it was OK. So in November and December I was seeing more things like this than I'd seen in the previous year and a half. I thought their relationship was really turning around."

Jamie struck me as entirely credible, although I always have a certain amount of skepticism about any informant. There's an element of romance in being involved in a great scandal or tragedy. We read about these kinds of things in the paper from time to time, we see the TV movies that are made about them, but to actually be a part of one!

There's a temptation, then, to make yourself a character, or a bigger character. Every actor wants a juicy part. So you start writing your own story, building up the importance of what you know. You don't change the facts, just the perspective, because you're the center now and what you know is what's important. And the story has to make sense from your point of view, from what you know.

Thera Huish's testimony is an even more dramatic example of this. Dan, of course, believes she simply lied repeatedly about his relationship with her daughter, in no small part because his murder conviction enabled Thera to keep Trish's half of T&T Enterprises. But assume for the moment her motives were less obvious. Thera knew Trish was her loving daughter, but, however repentant, Trish once had rejected her for Dan. Trish had committed this greatest sin against her mother with Willoughby, and she continued to sin by not repudiating him entirely. Psychologically, her punishment had to be related to that fatal flaw. Thera knew Willoughby was the devil, so she knew for certain, without the need to sift through evidence, that he had murdered her daughter as his final act of desecration.

Kay Lines' perspective, although his own, aligns perfectly with Thera's. Dan's guilt is by far the most convenient solution available to him. On a professional level, Lines knew that, if the murder had been a random act of violence by itinerant thieves, it would remain unsolved. On the other hand, sixty percent of all murders involve spouses, and the process of subtraction pointed you right at the guilty one.

I knew, I know ... what? Now, you may know a lot about an event, and it may all be true; you're not lying and you haven't been deceived. But what you know may not explain what really happened in that split second when someone — Dan or Yesenia, or both — stepped through the mirror. When he/she changed the world by murdering Trish Willoughby.

"Is a murderer so different from you and me?" I ask Frenchy.

"I was in the war," he shrugs. "A soldier is just a murderer by accident."

A murderer by accident: I'm not sure what he means, but it is a phrase that bonds me to Willoughby, to his story. Other guilty men seem able to make clear, moral distinctions. I cannot.

For the most part, we discover things about each other by accident; investigation or analysis occur after the fact, to confirm or rationalize. This is true even about those to whom we are closest, to the people upon our understanding of whom everything depends. It is true about our understanding of ourselves.

What did Dan understand about Trish when he married her? That she was attractive and lively and subject to his charms, willing to experiment with drugs and sex, that she was easy to spend time with and made few demands he was unable to meet with an acceptable amount of effort? What was left to be discovered by accident over the years was that Trish's eagerness to please him was in direct conflict with her eagerness to please others as well, particularly her mother, and the gravitational pull Thera Huish generated turned out to be the more powerful of the two. Dan must have been stunned when he realized that the values he had assumed his wife shared turned out to be values Trish had adopted for a time but which were not crucial to her. What was crucial was stability, and that could be based in a mother's love as well as a husband's, in her own financial activities as well as his.

And what did Dan know of his own daughter, Marsha? By 1988, when the Willoughbys adopted her at the age of fourteen, she'd been in thirteen different foster homes. Dan and Trish saw her on a TV news story called Wednesday's Child.

According to Dan, Trish was against adopting a teenager at first. Even after she grew to love her, Trish had a tough time dealing with Marsha's "rebel side." Dan suggested it was because Marsha reminded Trish of herself as a teenager.

Jamie told me that Marsha put up a lot of walls, as you might expect of someone with that kind of history. Never before secure in her environment, used to relationships that might last a few months or even less, Marsha was hard to get to know. But she seemed to be making progress with the Willoughbys, and with Jamie, who, although nominally her babysitter, was not yet thirty when Marsha turned sixteen. Jamie figured Marsha had some learning disabilities, at least an attention deficit disorder that kept her from focusing on anything for more than a few minutes at a time. To help her with her homework, Jamie would sit her at a table in a closed room with no distractions; yet, if she left for even five minutes, Jamie would return to find Marsha in fantasyland. She had problems with both basic math and reading, but seemed to be making progress in the more important area of her relationships, realizing for the first time what it meant to be a member of a family. Jamie thought she was making progress getting some of those walls down when Trish was murdered.

I asked Jamie if Marsha had trouble telling reality from fantasy. Jamie said no, her fantasizing was just a defense mechanism. I asked if Marsha had trouble judging time, if she'd really know how long the children sat in the driveway while Dan went back into the beach house, and she said that Marsha might not know because she probably just wouldn't have cared. Marsha sat for as long as she wanted, a few seconds or half an hour, and got up and wandered off when she wanted without thinking about it. Her conversation was the same way.

"Did you ask her point-blank about how long they were in the driveway?" I asked.

"Marsha was very selective about what she allowed herself to say, even to me. I couldn't tell if she really had no idea, or if she'd ducked behind one of her walls and was looking through it at me, wondering what I really wanted to know."

"Do you think she lied on the stand?"

"I would never consider Marsha a liar. She would avoid talking about it before she would lie. I know if Marsha tells me about it, it's the truth. I don't mean like, if she says, yeah, Jamie, I'll run to the store and she blows it off. If I ask her a serious question, she might try to avoid answering, but if she tells you something it's the truth."

"And if she doesn't want to talk about something?"

"Instead of telling you that, she'd say she didn't remember."

"So what did she tell you about the day of the murder?"

Jamie told me pretty much what she'd told the lawyers at her deposition. After the murder, it became very obvious to her that the Huish family was going to try to pin the murder on Dan. Dan became very protective about whom he allowed the children to spend time with. He worried about what everyone was telling them, including Jamie, who had been known to him, up to that point, only as Trish's friend and employee, as well as Thera's. She had to prove to him that her concern was for the children and that she wasn't acting as a spy for his deadly in-laws. "Once he accepted that, he let me be closer to the children, to spend time with them alone, but it was agreed between us that I would never pressure any of them into talking about it if they didn't want to."

"Did Marsha change her story for the police? They reported that she did."

"I don't know what she told them, in private or on the stand. I was excluded from the trial."

"Because you were a potential witness?"

"Right. And especially because I told the prosecution that Thera was lying through her teeth about Trish and Danny's relationship."

"About Trish and Danny breaking up, you mean?"

"Right. If Thera had that conversation with Trish, it certainly never showed up in the office. The things we talked about were things that you do when you're trying to heal a relationship, not to end it."

I asked about the relationship between Trish and Marsha. After all, Dan has let slip the fact that she was originally opposed to adopting the teenager.

Jamie said her most atypical memory of Trish, during the entire time they worked together, concerned an episode in November of '91, just three months before her murder, when Trish became extremely angry with Marsha. Something had been going on between them all day, and Trish was trying to talk to her on the phone about it. Suddenly she slammed the phone down, ran out to the long driveway in front of the family residence, jammed her car in reverse so that the tires squealed all the way out into the street. When Jamie saw her again, an hour later, the frustration and anger were gone, the problem apparently resolved. Jamie couldn't tell me what it had been.

I kept this image of Marsha for years — until I heard the prosecution announce at one of Dan's post-conviction hearings that Marsha was to take the stand to contradict her testimony at trial. Despite having watched Marsha socializing with the Huishes for many hours, seeing the way in which she was very much part of their clan, I was surprised. Marsha's story might determine Dan's life, and now she was going to change it? I wasn't the only one who was shocked; despite her protestations that she had considered the possibility of perjury and was unconcerned (because the prosecution assured her that, as long as she said what THEY wanted, she'd never be prosecuted for it?), Judge Howe adamantly refused to allow her to testify until she was represented by independent counsel. That testimony still has not been given.

Finally, what did Dan understand about Yesenia when he began their affair? That she found him exciting, that she was great in bed (and convinced him he was), and that her need for emotional commitment was as malleable as her schedule? She needed money, as "free" spirits often do, but he could handle that, at least for a time. What Dan didn't know about Yesenia made headlines.

He met her because he had to stop for a red light next to a bus stop where Yesenia and a girlfriend had just missed their connection. They approached Dan, gesturing for him to role down his window, and told him they had to get to Los Arcos Mall. As it happened, Dan was on his way to a business meaning just around the corner from there, so he agreed to give the women a ride. They asked what he did, and when they heard he was in international freight, Yesenia asked if he ever worked in Mexico. Dan had been thinking about expanding his company's business down there to try to capture some of

the freight traffic from the American compies, like Ford, G.E., and Westinghouse, that had started manufacturing goods down there to be shipped back to the U.S. Yesenia was well-dressed, attractive, and articulate, and Dan thought she might be able to open doors in Mexico that a gringo could not.

This is a light resume in the usual sense, although less so for lovers than, for instance, for babysitters.

"But why did he pick her up in the first place?" Carole has asked.

"Why did Hugh Grant pick up that hooker in LA?"

"So, you're saying men pick up any women they think will have sex with them?"

Dan in fact denies sex had anything to do with it. Maybe he's just a lot different from me. Without getting myself into trouble (ha!), I tried to explain at some length how men are more complex than that, blah, blah, blah.

"So, he was hoping to get laid?" Carole interrupted, unimpressed.

"It's not that simple. Men have sexual fantasies they don't necessarily believe in, but sometimes we act on them anyway. So you pick up a woman at a bus stop because you'd like to sleep with her, but you don't really expect it to happen, or even try to make it happen."

"So what made Yesenia special?"

"She said yes."

I understand Willoughby as a man having a classic mid-life crisis. He hated his job, he was getting older and saw his future opportunities narrowing to a pinhole. He learned that Yesenia had been married twice, and, when he learned the second divorce had never been consummated, he financed the paper work. He even met, and, before the trial, had thought he was on friendly terms with, at least one ex-husband. But by all accounts, Dan's first clue that Yesenia Patino had begun life as a male was when he was bluntly informed of the fact by the prosecutors who were, at the time, in the middle of accusing him of murder.

Dan denies my theorizing. He points out that he was at the top of his career when he quit his job and that he was looking forward to playing Mr. Mom. He was happy Trish was finally achieving her dreams in the business world (after several failed attempts he had helped finance). From my experience, however, I find my hindsight is better when I'm looking at events that actually occurred rather than remembering feelings I think I had.

Cops understand how little we really know about each other, and often turn that to their advantage. Think about the diabolical shrewdness of this interrogation strategy. You're sweating some guy in an interview room, without a lawyer present, because, hey, he tells you he's innocent so what does he need a lawyer for? You ask him about his relationship with Yesenia, his relationship with his wife ("Hey, who doesn't want a little on the side, right? We're all guys here."), what he knows about his wife's business and her insurance policies, if he ever hit or pushed around his wife ("Hey, we all do, buddy, when they piss us off. You're not saying you're better than us, are you?"), asking him what exactly he did every minute of the day on that date down in Rocky Point a month ago. Dan claims he's doing his best to cooperate, but you have his eyes shooting all over the room trying to locate the last thing he said which you're telling him isn't quite consistent with the second last thing he said. He won't budge on a crucial detail, on the first step you want him to take toward a confession. He won't tell you, for instance, yeah, I talked with Yesenia about killing Trish, but I was only kidding.

"You talked about a lot of kinky stuff with Yesenia, didn't you, Dan?"

"Well, I don't know. What do you mean by kinky?"

You snort, matter-of-factly. You turn the tape recorder off, like you're doing him a favor. "Come on, Danny boy. You know kinky. You were fucking this guy for a couple of years."

"What guy?" asks Dan.

"*Yesenia*, Dan. Don't tell me you didn't know she was a he? You want me to believe you're so damn dumb you didn't even know you were fucking a *guy*?" Casually you toss photocopies of Yesenia's medical records on the table revealing that she had a sex-change operation back in 1984.

Imagine Dan sitting in that room, cut off from reality but up until now able to reassure himself that it existed just on the other side of those walls. And then, BAM, like he's shot out of a gun, flying away from the center of his known universe at light speed, receding into a pinpoint in time and space.

Dan narrowly avoided this scene, because Ochoa learned of the sex change from the prosecution and was able to tell Dan just before both the Huishes and the cops sprung the news on him.

But in the meantime, when Dan regains the power of speech, he's got to be thinking: how can he say anything you will believe? He can't afford to hold anything back if he wants to have the slightest chance. Hell, maybe he should even tell you things he knows you want to hear, even if they're not entirely true. Now you flick the tape recorder back on.

"Of course we don't know anything about anyone else," Carole told me the other day before she herself went missing. "We don't want to. People never look each other in the face. Never listen. That's why t-shirts have all the cool stuff written on the back." All we want is a memorial line when it's over. The back of a t-shirt is the moment's tombstone.

"If you really want a man to pay attention to something," Carole added over her shoulder as she walked away, back to the kitchen for more limes, "a woman ought to print it on the seat of her pants."

I don't think our ignorance is quite so willful. We would know each other if it weren't too much trouble. But like light, people appear to be both particle and wave, depending on the perspective of the observer. You try to predict a person's reactions based upon the complex of forces operating at a certain point in time, or you try to predict his reactions by examining the wavefront of his personality generated from the depths of his genetic and social history — and have an equally good chance of being wrong. Apologies to Heisenberg, but it is only when someone already has acted, when the Schrodinger's cat box is open for all to see, that the pundits can explain to you "why" someone did what they did.

Siegel

Chapter 11: Local Law, Extra Crispy

Frenchy and Don are making pancakes and Bloody Marys. I have a couple of each and decline another invitation to go diving, submitting that I have to wait around for Carole to return, although I have no idea from where.

It is a beautiful morning in Rocky Point, the sea breeze a child's breath, the air not yet infected with the knowledge of humidity. In the blue-grey salt-sown atmosphere, my mind is beached blubber, breathing hard, wondering only vaguely how the hell it got here. Bev and Don start packing their gear as I try to unpack my thoughts and discover that, what the hell, I can get stinking drunk three days in a row. With no more than a questioning look, Frenchy and I are out the door.

But first he has a surprise for me, a visit to the local constable, Agustin, a source of great wisdom on all things criminal. I am already hip to the distinction between the Federales, Sly Brown's shock troops whom no one trusts, and the local law, for whom Los Gringos have both affection and respect.

I am glad Frenchy is there to lead me through the swamp of local dwellings we circumnavigate to reach the docks. I had imagined the locals lived among more elemental materials than the complex polymers in which Americans encase themselves, but there is nothing simple or appealing about these one-room shacks of mud, cardboard, and corrugated sheet metal. A poor life can be as complicated as a wealthy one, only it's likely to be shorter, and damn uncomfortable.

At the bottom of the delta of twisted, sand-packed streets, Agustin's police station is a shack on the dock next to an even more run-down shack that is home to the most disreputable looking fishing guides since Ahab. Pointing at the beaten boat and its unwashed crew of bleary-eyed, gap-toothed misfits, I ask Frenchy if he knows the percentage of patrons who actually return from their outings. He shrugs, as if it's a perfectly reasonable question which sadly requires more calculation than he is prepared to do.

Inside, a tallish brown man past middle age is bent over a shortwave radio, which, along with a map on the wall, are the only indications that this might be a police station. The illusion is not enhanced when the somber, long-faced, khaki-clothed man, whom Frenchy introduces as Agustin, hands me a business card announcing that he also delivers Kentucky "Style" Fried Chicken. The phone number is good for both his businesses, he says in Spanish, although police work is not mentioned on it.

With Frenchy acting partly as interpreter, partly as cultural ambassador, I proceed with the interview, hoping to learn a few objective facts which the prosecution pointedly ignored and Willoughby's own incompetent attorney failed to develop. I'd like to know, for instance, the extent of the search that was carried on for the murder weapon and the likelihood of it being found if it had been buried or flung into the sand or dropped into one of the construction dumpsters.

Also interesting to me is the extent of the splattering on the furnishings and walls of the murder room observed by the crime scene investigators. My sources in the States have assured me that whacking someone in the head with a mace hard enough to fracture her skull would be a very messy affair, equivalent to Gallagher hitting a watermelon with a sledge hammer, and that they'd expect the room to be covered with projectiled blood. It is clear, however, that Willoughby emerged from the house immediately after the prosecution claims he committed just this act without a trace of blood on his clothing, and no bloody clothing was ever located by the police. While Marsha's testimony is equivocal on many things, as a student of cosmetology she is obsessive about hair and clothing and is absolutely certain that Dan wore the same clothes in and out of the house and that he was perfectly clean upon emerging. Perhaps the prosecutor would argue the towel Dr. Lowry found draped over the victim's head had shielded him from flying brain matter, but this argument hangs, it seems to me, on the extent of spattering found elsewhere in the room.

Before Agustin will talk, I have to decline the fried chicken, a greasy, unmarked box of which appears from an open shelf beneath the radio, as if that contraption doubled as a microwave. I'd be mad not to decline. So little do the charred and battered hunks of flesh resemble chicken parts that I wonder if "fried chicken" is more of a euphemism than a cooked bird down here.

Because Agustin speaks only a little English, and I know I can rely on Frenchy being properly polite for me, I am as direct as possible. My first discovery, however, is that Agustin wasn't even involved in the murder investigation himself. I stare at Frenchy for a moment, who in turn prods Agustin in Spanish, and am told Agustin does at least know the cops who were involved, as well as the paramedics and the coroner. Because I am a friend of Frenchy's, he promises to make inquiries about how much blood there was on the walls and to get back to me. I hope that doesn't mean I will have to deal with the Mexican phone system.

"He is very, very good," Frenchy reassures me as we escape the fried chicken radio shack. Bev has told me the same thing, and Agustin's police work is one of the few topics Rex and Don seem to agree on. "He can track a barefoot man on a crowded beach for miles. And he's a great judge of character," Frenchy adds of his friend who has just told me that Willoughby looked guilty to him. At a local cantina, Frenchy and I stop for a few drinks so he can tell me some more things about the Italian-style diner he ran back in Pennsylvania with his dead wife. We debate the virtues of red versus white sauces. Frenchy smiles politely to a few of the other locals; he is not one of those men who judges his success by being known by more people than he knows himself. When we talk about Willoughby, he is most concerned not with Willoughby's dead wife but with the children finding the body.

The margaritas are the green of stagnant memories. I'm a heavy drinker and twenty years younger, but something in Frenchy, perhaps the rightness of his grief, absorbs the alcohol before it ever reaches his brain. I wish there was something in me that absorbed things before they got to my brain. But Frenchy is the most capable griever I have ever met. I simply am not of that caliber. I am only good at feeding my disease.

"By the way," I say finally, with the (for Rocky Point) heretical gesture of looking at my watch, "my own wife may not be dead," and explain that I have to get back. As Frenchy and I approach Bev's dune from one direction (having only been gone about three hours total), I see my car, pulling away without me in the other. Frenchy, who has been idealizing his own wife for the past hours, nevertheless gives me one of his shrugs and a little laugh and suggests it is time for me to work up an alcoholic sweat. As I jog down the sandy road, my stomach awash with margaritas, I wave my arms at the slowly retreating Camry and once again ransack my limited library of apologies for being gone all afternoon. But the car doesn't stop. As the Camry reaches the bottom of the sandy road leading from Bev's cluster of beach houses and hits a brief stretch of packed dirt, it accelerates toward town and is soon lost in that pocked, rutted, and rusted maze.

Panting and sweating, slowly I retrace my footsteps to where Frenchy is waiting on Bev's veranda. If his battered Stetson were fashioned from giant leaves, he would be perfect for this scene of an ancient shipwreck survivor appraising a new arrival. "Looks like you will have to stay for a while, amigo," he says, producing an extra Tecate, brown bottle glistening like a native's belly and handing it down to me. Then his broad, bearded face bursts out with a roar of laughter.

We sit on the stoop drinking and Frenchy tells me how it is to live in Mexico. As Frenchy and I sip our beers and stare thoughtfully from the concrete veranda in front of the suddenly empty beach house, Frenchy asks me about my book. As far as I can tell, Frenchy is no great reader, but has an outdated respect for writers.

"How long you been writing it?"

"Hard to say. Started the first time about two years ago. Now I'm starting again."

"What was wrong with the first time?"

"The words all seem dead to me... . I'm not really interested in telling the story I thought I was telling."

Frenchy's puzzled expression makes me feel guilty. My evasiveness is a disservice to Writers Everywhere. "See, at first I thought I was writing a book about a spectacular murder. But Carole and I have been having these problems, and now every time I think of Willoughby, I think of my own marriage...."

"I'm sorry," he says, and I nod my thanks, for that and for the fresh beer he hands me. I was already drunk from the margaritas, but chasing my wife's car and my ghosts has made me thirsty. "Maybe this is not the book you want to write."

His comment is so perceptive that I can only shrug in evasion. I wonder if Frenchy is ambivalent about his wife's death at some level. Not ambivalent in the sense that he wouldn't wish her alive again if he could. But each life we love is a burden. Every day is salted with a measure of fear that a loved one will be hurt. Every day is a struggle to protect your love from the world, and from yourself. Perhaps even Frenchy felt some relief in finally letting go of his wife, perhaps some great blood-sigh swelled up from the bottom of his being, through his lungs, and lifted off the top of his head.

Eventually he asks if I know how the Willoughbys felt about each other.

"Depends whom you talk to." I explain the prosecution's version of their relationship. There was no real evidence of any violence between the couple prior to the murder, although the prosecutor had assured the host of a local radio show to the contrary. The Willoughbys had had a few spats, and nearly broken up the summer before the murder when Dan finally told Trish about Yesenia.

"How did he tell her?"

"Apparently he discussed it with Marsha first. Then, when she failed to tell her mother, he came right out with it himself." Frenchy makes a sound of disgust. I feel a familiar shame. "Anyway, after the damage was done, he changed his mind about leaving, decided they should stay together for the kids' sake. Dan says he'd ended the relationship with Yesenia, but still felt responsible for her, and was trying to get her back to Oregon with her husband, Mielke. And he and Trish were making good progress at getting back together. The prosecutor said that Dan was still paying her rent and never intended to break up with Yesenia, that the whole reconciliation bit was just a trick to allay suspicion while he plotted to murder her."

"What do you think?" Frenchy asks.

I shrug. "Like any man, he wanted it both ways. He wanted his house and kids and his marriage and financial security, and he also wanted to screw strange women. He wanted his family to be happy, and he wanted the excitement of his love affair with Yesenia. So he told his wife he was breaking it off, and maybe he meant to, but, if he told Yesenia that, he didn't do it very convincingly. Dan was still paying Yesenia's rent in the fall, after the reconciliation thing had started. He took her to Rocky Point in early December, supposedly to break the news to her gently or to confirm that this was absolutely their last fling together, or whatever men think they're doing when they desperately want what they've told themselves they shouldn't have."

"He actually brought Yesenia to see the beach house he was renting for his family in February?" Frenchy repeats dubiously.

"Dan says it was a visual aid to explain why he couldn't see her again. The prosecution says that he brought her there to set up the murder."

"A *visual* aid?" Carole would snort in disgust. "How about a marital aid? An extra-marital aid?" I miss her already.

"You'd have thought up something better, wouldn't you?" Frenchy says, as if standing in for her.

Without actually thumbing through the history of my own deceptions and self-deceptions, I assure him I would have. Because it is so lame, it is one of the details of Willoughby's story that I can't make work as a lawyer, although as a lover, that is as a man whose scruples are no more than shadows cut from paper and pasted to the wall of his bedroom, I understand completely. He had a stable relationship with his family that afforded him psychological and financial security, a place to return to, and he also had a passionate, exciting relationship that assured him in that most convincing of whispers that he was not old, that he hadn't lost everything wild he'd ever felt running through his veins. Willoughby did not have the stomach to give up either of his lives. He had no intention of abandoning his affair with Yesenia; he was keeping her in his confidence in the matter of this vacation, but he had no real plans to resolve anything in her favor either.

"What's Yesenia getting out of it then?" Frenchy asks dubiously. "Just the rent?"

"I'm not saying she didn't think he was promising more. But what if," I allow myself slowly, "Dan doesn't see that Yesenia sees herself as more central to his life, because he doesn't want to see that? What if he didn't really plan to murder his wife, but he and Yesenia played this little mind game about it that only she took seriously? What if one of them suggested it, and they started developing a murder scenario to spice up their affair. It's a sex game from his side, but who knows how clear that is to Yesenia? The last thing either of them wants to believe is that their relationship will end."

Frenchy ponders this, knowing better than I that, in the end, there will be an end, to this relationship and to all of them. People have ideas, but they don't seem to have a plan. In the end, I will remember staring for the first time into the lenses of your eyes, thick as stargates, and will realize, finally, for the first time, that you were looking inward. It will be in the waning moments of our relationship, similar to the time period between giving your computer the command to shut down and receiving the message back that it is now safe to do so, so that this information will come to me, as always, not as real news but as a after-image of something I already know. My mind will hold only the shadow created by the persistence of vision after the screen has gone dark. You were always staring inward. So was I.

Frenchy is gone, and I have found a martini in my hand. "Christ," I mumble, "how purple can a guy get," and turn around, right into My Imaginary Girlfriend. At first I think it's another of her bizarre make-up games. Then, looking more closely, I wonder if perhaps bruises are considered cool. But as she moves to the wall at my side, she limps enough for me to notice.

"Hey. Are you OK?"

"No." She sips her beer, but even that seems to hurt.

"Did you fall off a jet ski, or what?" Then I see the fingerprints on her arm. I know how those are made. "Who the hell did this?" I can afford to be outraged. My wife's not here.

"He accused me of being a whore."

"Who did?"

"Stevie. My husband."

I pretty much inhale the olive from my martini, then have to blow it out of my esophagus. It hits the patio wall four feet away with a soft thump. "Your --"

She twists her fist into my collar to shut me up, and leads me further down the patio, into an available corner. I am trying to recall if this is our first, actual physical contact.

"You're married?" I finally manage, somewhat more casually. "And he's here with you?"

"Down there." She gestures toward the beach with her head. "There's a tent, a tent city, with some of his friends. A couple of the girls were here the first night you came, but they got bored."

"What about your husband?"

"He's cute."

"Intriguing, but not exactly a biography."

"Too cute, stuck up about it. So I wouldn't fuck him, so he asked me to marry him, and because I really wanted to fuck him, I said yes."

"I see. And he beats you up?"

She shrugs.

"Do you want to go back to him? Do you want to have him arrested? Do you want to hire an Italian to swap out his dick and his tongue, pardon my French? Give me a clue. What's your name, anyway?"

She takes the rest of my martini, tips her head back, and drains it, including the olives. I watch them go down her beautifully taut open throat, wending their way among the purple fingerprints. "Sophie."

I think about that for a moment and decide it makes as much sense as any other answer. "Has he beaten you up before?"

"He pushes me around sometimes, when I get jealous of all the other women hanging around him. But not like this."

"So what exactly brought this on?"

"My coming back naked last night."

"Ah," I say, recalling the t-shirt stuffed in my bureau drawer.

"I was up at the house for a shower. You know, I didn't exactly have permission, so when I thought I heard someone coming back, I kind of panicked?"

"Running outside naked seems like a lot of panic," I venture.

"Well, at home I don't wear clothes much. I just wasn't thinking about it. Then when I came back later, to -- where I left my shirt, I couldn't find it."

We both contemplate that for a moment. "So what are you going to do now? Do you want me to ask Bev and Don if you can sleep on the couch tonight?"

She shakes her head emphatically. "They've done too much for me already. I'll just have to go back down there and work it out."

"I'll come with," I announce, almost as if I mean it.

"Will you?" she begs, not what I had expected at all. "Maybe you can explain it to him. You're so smart, a lawyer and a writer and everything."

Before I have time to think what a fucking unbrilliant plan this is, we are walking down the beach, toward Sandy Beach, where the gringo tourists camp. The sunset is glaring across the water to my right, the moon has already risen up ahead. Our shoulders touch as we walk in the uneven sand. She isn't limping now, but reaches for my arm, to steady herself, I guess. But she doesn't let go after that. The evening is coming on, and we'll have to give up looking soon....

As Sophie's hand tightens on my bicep, I see someone approaching along the shoreline, coming on steadily out of nowhere like a migraine headache. He is tall, dark, and slim, in his early twenties, more arabic than hispanic, and as good-looking as one of those underwear ad guys I see in Carole's **Vanity Fair** magazines I peruse while taking a crap. He's a little tougher looking than I'd hoped.

He doesn't look at me for more than a split second. "What are you doing back here?" he asks Sophie. "I told you I never want to see you again. And where the hell have you been all morning anyway?"

"Hey," I say, putting aside my personal need to deal with some of these contradictions. "There's been a misunderstanding here."

"You the old guy she's fucking?" he snorts, still looking only at Sophie.

"Of course not," I protest, as if astounded by the notion.

"What if he is?" Sophie screams back.

"I am not!" I protest.

"Right, fatso," says Stevie, "why don't you fuck her in the ass? Then I'll fuck her too. Sloppy seconds for her own husband!"

"You want sloppy seconds, Stevie?" Sophie's voice is a quiet snarl. "Just stick your tongue in this ear and that gun in my other ear and pull the fucking trigger!"

I don't see a gun, and now I decide I'd better close the distance between us before he pulls one out and I'm too far away to make a grab for it.

"The law says I could kill you both," Stevie informs me with a pointed finger as I advance. "If a man catches his wife --"

"We're not really married. That fake license you got may have fooled your parents --"

"You told him that!" the man/boy howls in rage. "I'll kick your ass so hard --"

"Try it, you little fuck!"

"Hey!" I try again, but they, we, are getting uncomfortably close to each other by this time. The surf is just a few feet to my right and his left, and I imagine the footing will be a little firmer close to the water line, important for a stud with aging ankle and knee joints. I edge over a step. "Leave the lady alone."

He looks at me appraisingly for the first time. "You gonna fight me, old man?"

"He's gonna kick your ass!" Sophie assures him.

"--Or you wanna wait until I get my father, and you can fight him?"

"Look sonny--"

"You look, Pops. This is none of your business. Unless, of course, you have been screwing her."

"No," I protest, "I haven't. But I can't let you beat her up either." I look up and down the beach, hoping someone will intercede. The strip is suddenly deserted, as if there's been a hurricane warning only I didn't hear.

"So stop me."

I sigh and step forward. I haven't been in a lot of fights, partly because I'm used to my bulk intimidating people, but this little shit is not intimidated, either, I think, because he knows how to fight or because he knows nothing about it. "Look," I try again.

"No, you look," the bastard shouts, and throws sand right in my eyes.

"He's got a black belt!" I hear Sophie shout, and wonder briefly which one of us she's lying about now as he crashes into me, his head smashing into the bridge of my nose in an explosion of pain.

Still, plowing into me is not a smart thing to do, as I outweigh him by fifty pounds and can now fight with my eyes shut. Even in my blind pain I'm able to get my arms around him so that we crash into the sand together, me on top, and the air whooshes out of him.

I try to open my eyes then, which proves to be a big mistake. While I'm distracted by the burning and thoughts of corneal damage, the little bastard wriggles away from me, and now I have to struggle to my feet and fight blind. I hear him still gasping for breath a few feet behind me, wheel so that my back is to the ocean and my feet planted solid, and risk one excruciating glimpse, just in time to see him coming right at me again -- he truly does not know how to fight -- and I discover then that I have come up with my own handful of sand, which, as I step aside, I fling in his direction like some cartoon mage. To my surprise, I hear him curse, and feel him miss, his body brushing by me as he stumbles into the surf.

So now the playing field is level; we are both fighting blind. Another glimpse and I see him hunched in calf-deep water, rubbing his eyes with wet, sandy hands, and I move in on him. He hears me coming in the surf and flails out in my general direction, and I reciprocate. I hear the punches whizzing through the air, but we are both missing, because both of us are trying to keep out of the other's range, until he grazes my cheek with a right hand, and the shock of it opens my eyes for a second.

And by now I'm plenty pissed. I rear back, then take a step forward, and nail him right in the face with a round-house right. He falls, spinning into two feet of water, and I throw myself on his back, my hands around his neck to strangle him in the surf, to hold him under until he drowns, and then I lift my right fist, mace-like, to smash his face again--

But he has stopped resisting, is merely flopping under me like a seagull with broken wings. I let him up, and crawl back out of the surf, trying to use a damp corner of my t-shirt to dab away any loose grains of sand which have not yet planted themselves permanently in my eyeballs. I hear him choking and gasping behind me, slowly following me out onto the beach, two gallapogos tortoises completing some ancient, incomprehensible, genetically encoded ritual.

That's when Sophie starts kicking him. She gives him a good shot in the ribs, and then, when he falls, drives her heel right into his face. I can't tell if the sound I hear is merely the impact of wet sand or his jaw breaking. By the time I get over there, she is on his back, clawing at his eyes with her fingernails, and he is whimpering and crying. As I pull her off, she rakes me across the cheek as well, and, in my current state, I jerk my hand back to smack her one, but I hear her gasp, and it's enough to stop me, so I just let her go. We stand there panting for a moment, me with my eyes closed. I can hear the boy groaning, but, uncharitably perhaps, I refuse to open my eyes to look at him, to see what we've done to his beautiful face. Then I feel Sophie's hands around my left arm, and she is pulling me back along the beach. I can feel her breast, through her wet t-shirt, pressed flat against the arm she is gripping. The nipple is erect. I am not.

"I can't see," I announce, so that she will not let go of my arm. "I've got to get to some fresh water. The salt just makes it worse."

"I know," she says, suddenly the professional nurse. "Your nose is all fucked up too. Bet it hurts." And when she reaches up and touches it, I let her know it does now. "I'll get you back to the house."

"Well, Bev and Don's...."

"You don't want all those people to see you bleeding?" She laughs, obviously exhilarated. "Wait'll I tell them how you fucked up Stevie!"

"I really rather you wouldn't. Tell anyone about this, I mean." Christ, I thought, what if Carole hears about this. She's always accusing me of backing down when her honor's at stake, usually after she's insulted some drunk in a bar or stolen someone's seat at a concert. If she finds out I actually got into a fist-fight over this teenager....

"I know another place," she says, and I can feel her start to move us inland."He should work out more, don't you think?"

"Stevie? How the fuck should I know? I'm old. For me, a good cough is exercise."

She laughs. She is exhilarated. She guides me up a set of stone steps, into another of the gringo houses. Thankfully, it is deserted. She leads me expertly to the shower. If we are breaking and entering, she's done it here before.

"Who's house is this?"

"Rex's." I should have recognized the sound of the wind on the water tanks, I suppose. "He'll be over at Bev and Don's for a couple hours, like every evening." She stands me under the nozzle and turns on the cold water, which is not that cold at this time of year. Still, I take a half step backward, right into her, before I realize she is still there, in her own wet and sandy t-shirt. Her small breasts press against my back.

"Sorry," I say.

"Work on your eyes first," she suggests. And I hear her stripping off her wet t-shirt. "God, there's so much sand."

"So, are you married to him or not?"

"I wouldn't be here in the shower with you if I was."

"But --" I feel her hands around the waistband of my swim trunks. I can't get anything like all the sand out of my eyes, but I am suddenly not noticing that much any more.

And then, before I can tell her no, sorry, I'm married and trying to work things out with my wife, I hear Rex's front door bang open.

Chapter 12: Blood Money

Dan Willoughby got the death sentence because prosecutors convinced the jury that he had murdered Trish for money, specifically for two insurance policies totaling a million dollars. The Arizona capital punishment statute also allows the death penalty in the case of a particularly heinous or brutal murder, and prosecutor Tom Mitchell argued that as well, but Judge Howe imposed the ultimate penalty because Dan supposedly killed his wife for the money.

Judge Howe is not known to shrink from imposing the death sentence, but the same defense attorneys that fear him for that also allow that he gives a defendant a very fair trial. The evidence that Dan killed Trish hoping to collect these insurance policies, however, was easily refutable — had Dan's attorney, David Ochoa, bothered to bring the appropriate witnesses at trial.

The allegation that Dan murdered Trish for the million dollars was first made by Thera Huish during her brutal civil law suit against Dan for control of Trish's share of T&T Enterprises. Because the law prohibits a murderer from inheriting anything from his victim, no one was surprised to see Thera attempt to freeze Dan out of the company by accusing him of murder even before she was willing to divulge the existence of the policies themselves. In the weeks after Trish's death, Thera was trying to claim the policies had insured Trish only as a "keyman" in T&T, and that Dan was never an intended beneficiary. Thera even was subject to counter-accusations that she had defrauded the insurance company as well as her own grandchildren in altering the terms of one of the policies after Trish's death. By the time of Dan's murder trial, when it was clear that he could not successfully maintain his civil lawsuit and fight for his life at the same time, she became unequivocal in her accusations that it was the insurance money that had motivated Dan all along — although she continued to spend it in direct violation of a court order, either because she truly believed the money had never been designated for anyone else or because she only recognized the law as her personal weapon. But clearly her accusations, advanced by the prosecution, make no sense. If Dan knew about the policies and Thera always was the intended beneficiary, how could Dan have profited by killing his wife?

Apparently, Thera Huish began inquiring about her daughter's insurance within days after her murder, while there is no evidence that Willoughby even knew, much less inquired about it for months. In her statement to the Mexican version of the Attorney General's Office, Thera swore that Dan had demanded this insurance money on the day of Trish's funeral. Dan states this is not only untrue but impossible, because he didn't even learn of the existence of the million dollars in insurance coverage until six weeks later.

The insurance agents who sold Trish and Thera the $250,000 and $750,000 policies would seem to be the logical sources for information in sorting out this controversy. The sale was conducted in private with mother and daughter, over the course of several business meetings in the months before Trish's death. The agents say that, initially, the two women were interested in these policies only for a "buy-sell" agreement for T&T Enterprises, essentially insuring that if one of them died, the other would have the money from the insurance to buy the other's share of the business from her estate. The women were still considering and reconsidering these policies in early December 1990 — when Willoughby already had rented the vacation beach house in Rocky Point. So if Dan had only rented the beach house in order to murder his wife for this insurance money, he was prescient indeed.

In it's summary of "facts," the Supreme Court stated bluntly that Dan had been involved in urging and arranging for these policies. However, there never was any direct testimony to that effect. When Dan's former secretary was asked if Dan knew anything about insurance for T&T, she said she thought he'd mentioned it, but Dan says the only time he ever suggested anything concerning T&T was when he urged Trish and Thera to incorporate in order to protect the Willoughby family home from creditors if the business ever was sued. This seems more likely, since Dan had not worked with his secretary for six months before either Trish or Thera inquired about insurance.

The agents themselves, Bob Bjerkin and Phil Guthrie, have both given sworn statements that neither of them told Dan or anyone else about existence of the policies, because Thera herself specifically instructed them not to. While Thera denied having issued this instruction under oath, Jamie Tepp, the only one outside of the Huish clan likely to have known about the insurance, clearly didn't. Dan claims he first learned of the $250,000 policy on May 7, 1991, from his own insurance agent, Jim Parker, with whom Dan and Trish both had had the same $20,000 life insurance package since 1986. Parker learned of the secret agreement between Huish, Bjorken, and Guthrie. When Dan expressed skepticism, Parker told him Beneficial Life had faxed him a copy of a check for $250,000 that already had been paid to Thera. Parker also filed a sworn statement which includes his belief that Dan never knew of these policies until he revealed them in their meeting months after the murder.

How Thera had managed to pocket this money so quietly while a murder investigation was still under way also is interesting. According to Dan and Guthrie, she did it by committing fraud, by having one of the insurance policies changed from a "buy-sell" designation, which required Thera to use the money to buy Trish's half of the business from Dan and his kids, to "key man" insurance, which paid benefits directly to Thera upon Trish's death. Guthrie says Thera approached him with this scheme shortly after Trish's death, and, when he refused to alter these legal documents, she filed a false complaint against him with the Arizona Department of Insurance. While this complaint was completely groundless, alleging such foolery as Guthrie hadn't completed his high school education, it took him months to have the complaint dismissed and might have clouded his credibility at trial.

Guthrie's testimony, and Bjorken's, would have been that Thera Huish, contrary to her trial testimony that "the policies were never kept secret from anyone," specifically had instructed them to do just that, and that neither of them had ever revealed their existence to anyone, including Dan Willoughby. Both agents say they believe Dan never knew of either policy until May 1991.

Debbie Schwartz, the same investigator for the prosecutor's office who rear-ended Dan on a freeway ramp while attempting to tail him, admits that she "visited with" Guthrie, but took no notes and didn't bother to tape-record the interview. Therefore, she claims, she never actually "interviewed" him and so never had to disclose this fact to the defense. That the very fact of the contact itself had to be disclosed under Brady was shrugged off as an oversight. Perhaps this single event arguably is nothing more than a conveniently narrow interpretation of the law. But, according to Guthrie, when Schwartz first attempted to get him to swear that Dan knew of the insurance money and he responded by telling her Thera Huish was a liar, she simply put away her notebook and decided not to record anything. This is consistent with an affidavit filed by another witness who turned out to be friendly to Willoughby, Jodene Critchfield. Ms. Critchfield, herself an experienced legal assistant, familiar with the legal interview process, was a close friend of both Dan and Trish for a number of years before the murder, and was appalled by the interview techniques used by Kay Lines and Schwartz when they interviewed her concerning potential trial testimony. Lines and Schwartz repeatedly turned their tape recorder off and on in order to ask leading questions and edit her responses to them. Ms. Critchfield felt they tried to coerce her into saying negative things about Willoughby that were either false or of which she simply had no knowledge. When no copy of the interview tape was provided to Ms. Critchfield, as the parties had agreed before the interview, she called the Attorney General's Office to request a copy — and was told it was "unavailable." She called both Lines and Schwartz repeatedly about the matter, but they never returned her phone calls.

Guthrie, like Critchfield, even contacted Ochoa about this matter, but again Dan's defense attorney never bothered to respond even though it was Dan's supposed knowledge of these policies that literally hung him. Nor did Ochoa ask the jury simply to work out the logic of this situation. If Dan and the insurance agents are telling the truth, Dan cannot have killed his wife for her insurance money because he didn't know it existed. On the other hand, if we speculate that Thera Huish is telling the truth because Trish privately told Dan about the existence of the policies, Dan still cannot have killed his wife for the "key man" insurance money because he would have known he could never be its beneficiary. Additionally, the prosecution's claim that Dan only rented the house in Rocky Point as part of a long-planned conspiracy to murder Trish is impossible, because the house was rented before Trish and Thera took out the policies. This fact alone could be fatal to Dan's conviction, because Arizona jurisdiction was predicated in part on the fact that the murder was planned in the Phoenix area, as evidenced by the beach house rental.

I have turned off Rex's shower, figuring this is not the time to piss him off by using up all his hot water, and am listening intently. There is not a sound in the house. I step out of the shower and pat dry my tenderized face. Sophie's latest t-shirt is gone. She has led Rex away, and I make my escape.

Chapter 13: Interviews

Bored with turning the cold, worn stone of the Willoughby case over in my hand again and again, I wander into Don's workshop. It is as capacious as Mexico itself, crammed with ancient tools, parts of tools, piles of tangled materials that bespeak an alien order, suggesting uses I would never have imagined for them. There are projects either half-built or half-broken down, but in either case looking like distinct possibilities not imagined (or imaginable) back in the States. I have learned that many of the half-built, roofless structures derelict upon the highways around here are not abandoned, as I had imagined, but works in progress by middle-class people who cannot afford the exorbitant interest rates charged by Mexican banks and so build piecemeal, a few dozen cinderblocks at a time, whenever they can afford those.

I try to make myself useful to Don, although, since he is both handy and an experienced engineer, that means mostly I stay out of his way and grunt appreciatively from time to time. We are discussing lunch when Rex shows up looking much the worse for wear. He has a black eye of his own and stitches in his swollen lower lip. Who knew these things were communicable even in Mexico? "Good meeting?" I ask innocently.

"Fucking Federale punched me because I said Brown was an ignorant sonofabitch. Federale said he was educated in the United States. Bastard never even got his goddamn GED, though."

"Actually," Don observes, "Rex asked if it wasn't a QED. Or maybe he did some graduate work and got a DDT. Federale didn't think that was humorous."

"He didn't know what I was talking about."

"But he knew you were making fun of him."

"What kind of third-world country is this where you can't make fun of the natives?"

"A Federale is not a native," Don sighs. "He's a delinquent with a license to kill. And for all you know, he punched you for some other reason, or no reason at all. That's what makes them so scary."

By the time lunch and noon beers drift by, Frenchy has joined me on the patio, and I roll my plot-rock toward him. No one says anything about my face, and I've covered the various scratches on my torso with a t-shirt allegedly displaying the dissected brain of a lawyer. Bev and Don's patio has become so familiar in the past few days that it has ceased to exist as *mis en scene* of any depth, is no longer even the mere backdrop for conversation, its crowd a cast divided into players and extras, but an extension of myself. I am no more conscious of it than of the shape of my hand or the color of my own eyes. Maybe I am camouflaged from the others by this same phenomenon.

Frenchy thinks that Willoughby's behavior right after the discovery of the bodies is pretty bad. "Acting guilty is one thing," he says. "But acting guilty when no one even accused you yet, that's bad."

"What if," I suggest to Frenchy, "there are more conspirators, not fewer?"

"Like who? The mother killing her to take over the business and get Willoughby out of the way at the same time?"

"No, not unless she hired someone. She was up in Phoenix when the murder occurred. I was thinking of the daughter, Marsha. What if she was in on it, and Willoughby panicked trying to cover up for her?"

"You think she's psycho or something?"

"I don't know." The shrug brings my beer to my lips. "Her foster care records are the place to look, but they're legally closed. She had an abused childhood, though, so the possibility she'd use violence against another family member is certainly greater than normal."

"When did she do it?"

"Well, the younger kids never testified about how long Marsha was back in the house while they waited in the Blazer. Or about whether she was carrying anything when she came out, or what she was wearing. Suppose she came back in and smashed her mother in the head with a statue or some other blunt object while Dan was in the bathroom. He comes out, stops her, but it's too late. She wraps the object in her bloody blouse, puts on a new one, and they go back out to the Blazer together. While the kids are in the museum, Dan loses the blouse and the murder weapon in the ocean."

"You think this guy would take the side of an adopted daughter against his own wife?"

"Well, he figures it's already too late to save the wife...."

"And?"

"Suppose they were lovers? She's over sixteen, probably plenty experienced at flirting with men after the early abuse and living in all those different foster homes. They're not really father and daughter, but they're together all the time.... If they're lovers, she's got a motive too."

"Woody Allen," Frenchy nods.

"She could give the Pillsbury Dough Boy a woody," Rex asserts as he sits down next to us.

"You've met Marsha?" I ask him, startled.

"Marsha who? I thought you were talking about —"

Before he could blab on about what he might have seen or heard the previous afternoon, I explain we are talking about Marsha, Willoughby's adopted daughter. To no one's surprise, Rex likes the theory. "It's perfect!" he says. "That's why Dan and Lolita —"

"Marsha."

"Dan and Marsha frame Yesenia! Dan sets Yesenia up by getting her on the scene, Dan and Marsha kill the mom together, and Yesenia is supposed to get caught holding the knife. She's a perfect fall guy. Fall fag. Whatever. She's so goddamn obvious, so highly visible, and she wouldn't have a clue about Marsha horning in on her man beforehand. Only something happens and Yesenia gets away despite herself. Then Dan has to lie about everything to save his own butt and Marsha's."

"Uh, that's pretty good," I admit, "but I was thinking more along the lines of proving this guy innocent."

"No man should be condemned to death for killing his wife," Rex opines. "He's already been condemned for life by marrying. Where's yours, Mack?"

"My wife?" I repress an inappropriately self-righteous impulse to criticize his lack of respect for my marriage, but realize I don't know.

A sudden absence, like an unseen animal darting from camouflage into complete cover, startles me as I pack up my pages and slide them back into the desk: the black t-shirt has vanished. I've been in the dark for so long, I realize, I think of fungus as one of the basic food groups. What does Carole think she knows?

According to Kay Lines, in the weeks following the murder, Dan recognized that the police were going to try to implicate him and Yesenia, panicked, and decided she should simply leave town for a while, to stay with her former husband Jack Mielke up in Oregon, what they both thought of as a "safe house." Dan denies this, pointing out that Yesenia's reunion with Mielke was so long planned that he had come to Phoenix months before the murder to pick up most of Yesenia's possessions. In any event, the night before she was due to fly to Oregon to meet Mielke, Yesenia was picked up and questioned by Lines, but released because there was still no evidence tying her to the murder. By the time a warrant was issued, she was in Mexico. Her disappearance gave Dan some breathing room to try to deal with his family and financial affairs, although he knew he was being followed on a daily basis by agents of the Attorney General's Office.

Maybe the prosecutors never would recover the homemade mace he'd used to shatter his wife's skull. There hadn't been an eyewitness and there was no physical evidence, no blood on Dan's clothing or anything like that. But they had Yesenia. She gave herself to the prosecutor the way she'd given herself to every useful man who asked-- on her own terms, in her own way, but gave herself, nevertheless. With Mielke, her first husband who had paid for her surgery, with Able Rascon, the second, convict stud, with Willoughby — and now with this gringo investigator Lines. She did it so casually, put up so little resistance, you'd have thought she'd get nothing but heartache and handcuffs. Maybe she thought she knew how to get what she wanted from men because she'd been one once herself.

Lines is one of the more aggressive investigators since Elliot Ness, known for relentlessly hounding everyone from witnesses to employees of other governmental departments when he doesn't get what he wants. Ostensibly operating as an investigator for the State, Lines had Gilbert police staking out Yesenia's apartment in Chandler long before there was any hard evidence against anyone. On the evening of March 3, the Gilbert cops reported that Yesenia apparently was moving out. Tony's pick-up and another were already being loaded. Armed only with a misdemeanor warrant on Yesenia for failure to appear in a City of Mesa Court on shoplifting charges years before, Lines ordered the Chandler police to make a traffic stop on the two pick-up trucks as soon as they left the apartment complex. Apparently untroubled by the illegality of stopping vehicles without reasonable belief that the drivers had done anything illegal — or, alternately, perhaps believing that any Hispanic with a pick-up truck full of household possessions was inherently suspicious, even when you had just watched them load up at a relative's house — the Chandler police rousted the drivers and forced them to produce the phone number of the woman for whom the furniture had been packed, a Victoria Mielke. Knowing Mielke was Yesenia's name by her prior marriage to Jack Mielke, Lines traced the number to Room 311 at the Airport Hilton.

Lack of a search warrant or the probable cause needed to obtain one didn't stop Lines here either. Persuading the hotel management to trick Yesenia into coming down to the hotel lobby to make an additional deposit on the use of her telephone, Lines and Detective Ruet of the Chandler PD confronted her as soon as she appeared there. When she denied she was Yesenia Patino, he demanded additional identification — knowing she'd left it up in her hotel room — which he had no cause to enter.

According to Lines, however, he only had to ask, and she invited him and Detective Ruet up to 311. There, also without coercion, she proceeded to tell him a detailed fiction about her life as Victoria, from her birth in Idaho, through her marriage to Jack Mielke of LeGrand, Oregon, whom she was about to rejoin. She'd come to Arizona to work, but had decided it wasn't good for their son to be without her. She had been Yesenia's roommate in Chandler, but Yesenia had returned home to Valle

Hermosa, Taumalipas, in Mexico, three months earlier to help care for her sick parents. Yesenia's husband, Abel Rascon, a Mexican national, sadly was in prison in Nogales for drug smuggling. "Victoria" told Lines she couldn't produce a driver's license because it had been revoked several years earlier for DWI: "I do love to drink," she laughed. Observing a rental car brochure on a nearby table, Lines asked her if she had any other ID — and, as soon as she reached into her purse, stopped her and had Ruet empty out the contents of the purse on the bed. He was entitled to do that to protect himself. How else could he have been certain she wasn't reaching for a gun?

From the purse, she produced, among other things, a valid passport under the name of Victoria Mielke. Technically, that should have ended the investigation that technically wasn't going on. But Lines was interested in some other things. One was a clothes catalogue with some phone numbers scrawled on the cover. "Is this yours?"

"Sure," she said, apparently oblivious to the fact that it was addressed to a Ms. Dan Willoughby.

"What about that Date-minder?"

"That was Yesenia's. She left it behind. I was going to send it to her."

"Have you ever been in trouble with the police?"

"No." She again laughed. "I probably would have been if I hadn't lost my license."

Lines, a Mormon teetotaler, of course, was not amused by confessions of drinking. When she again denied having seen Yesenia for the past month, he warned her it was a crime to give false information to the police. She was confused to hear Lines refer to himself as "the police," having assumed his status with the Attorney General's Office made him a lawyer. He only replied that he was an investigator.

"You fit the description we have of Yesenia Patino yourself," Lines told her.

"I do? Well, she did look a bit like me. People thought we were sisters."

Lines questioned her about where she'd been employed, and then asked to look at the wedding ring she wore, a gold band with multiple stones that looked like diamonds.

"Victoria" finally asked Lines what the matter was he had come to inquire about. Lines told her that he was looking at a friend of Yesenia's named Dan as a suspect in a very serious crime.

"What did Yesenia do?"

"Probably nothing. We just want to talk to her so she can tell us about this guy, this Dan."

She said she'd never heard of him.

"Who did you see when you were living with her."

"A lot of different men came by. She hung out in a lot of Mexican places."

"This was a white guy."

"No, I don't remember any white guy."

Lines and Ruet exchanged looks, and left the room together to confer in the hallway. Lines came back in alone and told her Ruet had gone to use a secure phone.

"Look," said Lines, finally, "I have a warrant for you from the Mesa Police Department. If you come with me, we can check their fingerprints and photographs, and if everything's OK, we'll bring you right back."

"What warrant?" She wondered if that was the right response, not realizing there was no right response to someone like Lines.

"For shoplifting, back on June 28, 1989."

She remembered the self-righteous assholes at the ABCO supermarket, all right, and that flustered her. "I took care of that problem. I went to Mesa court and I paid that, for the uh, for that shoplifting. I took care of that problem." This definitely is not the right response.

"What name were you using then?"

"Victoria ... Mielke."

"We need to check on this warrant."

"There's a mistake. I took care of that."

"The warrant is confirmed."

"I had a lawyer."

"What's his name?"

"But he took care of it.... I don't want to go to any police station. Can't you just call or something?"

"Do you know Dan Willoughby?"

"No. I never heard of the guy."

"Who picks up the mail at your apartment?"

"Well, I do."

"Ever get any for Yesenia — or for anyone named Willoughby?"

Yesenia was so lost in her lies by then that she was no longer even hesitating. "Yes. For both of them."

"But I thought you told me you never heard of the guy."

"I meant I never met him, never saw him. But there was mail for his name, and for the names Yesenia Patino and for Yesenia Rascon."

"Didn't you ever ask her about him?"

"Once. She just said he was a guy she used to go out with."

"Then why is his mail coming to your address?"

"You'll have to ask her."

Lines sighed, consulted the ceiling, looked back at her. "Look, if you were Yesenia, is there some reason you wouldn't tell us?"

"Why should I say that's me when I know it's not me?"

"Detective Ruet's been on the phone for the last ten minutes. Any second now he's going to come back in here and tell me who you really are. And I'm going to be mad, because I've wasted a lot of time. Now, I just want to know about this guy Willoughby."

"Why? What for?"

"Dan's wife got murdered. It's been in all the newspapers. You didn't hear about that?"

"Un-uh. When did that happen?"

"Not long ago."

"So if Dan murdered his wife, I don't know if he did or not, but if he did.... Do you have any evidence?"

"More than we're going to tell you about."

"I don't have any information about Mr. Willoughby, OK? I mean, I know him some, but I didn't know the wife got murdered and I don't know him well enough to say he killed her or had any reason to."

Lines didn't say anything.

"Where did this murder happen?"

"Rocky Point. Didn't you read about it in the paper?"

"I told you, I don't know anything about it...."

"Did you go to Mexico with Willoughby?"

"Yes, I have gone to Mexico with Dan Willoughby a couple of times." *SMASH-CUT CLOSE-UP IN SLOW-MO! Without ever admitting that she was Yesenia, Yesenia became her again, or some version of her. And Lines just never mentioned the transition, never asked her again to admit it.*

"Where'd you go?"

"Cancun. And we went to Mazatlan, and Cabo San Lucas."

"When was that?"

"About ... within this last year."

"What months."

"May or June."

"You ever meet his wife?"

"Uh-huh. Her name was Trish."

"Did Dan ever talk about getting a divorce, or leaving her for some reason, anything like that?"

"No. He never said that."

"You two were pretty good friends?"

"He said he was happy with his wife and kids. And they were very active in the Mormon church. He invited me to come to the Mormon church a couple times."

Has she caught on to something, he wondered? "Did you go?"

"No, I studied that church. They were too pushy, wanting to control everything you do."

So no, she hadn't. "When was the last time you saw Dan?"

"About two weeks ago. He came over to the house and said he was going to take his wife and the kids over to Mexico. I asked where, and he said he didn't know whether to take them to Nogales or Rocky Point. When I asked him for how long, he said just the weekend. It was his Christmas package for them to go and have a good time in Mexico."

"But you haven't heard anything about the murder?"

"Un-uh. No, I told you, I didn't read about it in the paper, and Dan didn't say anything."

"When was the last time you were in Mexico?"

"About three weeks ago. I went on a Thursday and came back Sunday." She tells him about visiting Abel in prison there, where he's been for over a year, since getting busted with five pounds of pot at the Agua Prieta border crossing.

"Do any traveling while you were down there?"

"A little. I went to Guaymas."

"Get to Rocky Point?"

"A couple of times. Me and my brother were in Rocky Point this last time." And she told him about her brother, Antonio Patino. She wanted to see some friends there and he had a truck, so she paid for the gas and they went together. They had a real good time, but got in some trouble on the way back, a Park Ranger pulling them over for speeding just after they crossed the border from Rocky Point. Because her brother was driving on a suspended license, they made them go back to immigration. They hassled her about lying when she crossed the border, but she had a passport so they had to let her go, especially *when she made them give her a paper to file a complaint. She still had the paper in her purse.*

Lines ignored the variation on the date, letting Yesenia's version drift back toward the continent of truth across the sea of might-have-been on its own accord. "Did you know Dan was down there?"

"Un-uh."

"Did you meet him down there?"

"Un-uh."

"Did you see him down there?"

"Un-uh."

"What's your brother like?"

Yesenia described him as two years younger than her 34, kind of quiet. He worked in construction, hanging sheetrock.

"When did they let you go through customs?"

"About six o'clock on Saturday. They didn't give me a ticket or anything."

"Do you remember the name of the agent you talked to?"

"There were three of them. They were pretty friendly," she noted with a flirtatious smile.

"So you haven't seen Dan since you got back?"

"Right."

"He hasn't called you or anything?"

"He called me here the other day, Friday. He said he wanted to take me out to lunch, but he never showed up."

Lines figured Willoughby must have made that call just before their own interview on that day, then thought better of meeting her in person when he knew he might be watched. "You see him regular?"

"Once a week," she shrugged. "I call him and talk to him or talk to his kids, or sometimes he'd call me."

"You teaching him Spanish?"

"Uh-huh."

"Is he any good?"

"Pretty fair," she smiled.

"Did you see Trish this last time in Mexico?"

"I didn't see any of them." She had a ball, got drunk, spent some time on the beach, went to see her friends, and partied.

"But you didn't see Dan?"

"I didn't think much about him. He's my husband back home, you know?"

"Not exactly."

"He's got his wife and kids there, he's happy with them, but he likes me to know I'm his wife too. I think he likes to say that because he's Mormon, you know, and can have more than one wife."

Lines loved this shit. "So you were going to marry him?"

"No way. That's a joke. I left Jack, my first husband, because he was a lot older than me. He's like 56. When I married Abel, he was younger than me, not even 28 yet. Dan, he's nearly as old as Jack, so why would I marry him?"

"Maybe because he's got money."

"I'd rather be happy with Abel than have money."

"But Dan's paying your rent, isn't he? Four hundred dollars a month?" The landlord had told him that.

"Yeah, but that's for.... I'm doing a lot of his paper work, and teaching him Spanish, like I said. He's very involved with his classes. I'm a teacher, you know."

"Are you?"

"I was a teacher's aide once. Part-time."

"Has Dan given you any money lately?"

"When I saw him last Friday he gave me $150. For Spanish teaching. For correcting his papers."

"Have you come into a lot of money in the last couple of weeks?"

"No."

"When you went to Mexico, you said you went to Nogales first, then to Rocky Point."

"Uh-huh."

"Did you know Dan was in Rocky Point?"

"No. He said he was either going to Nogales or to Rocky Point, so I didn't know."

"Did you look for him down there?"

"I went to this one place, Manny's, where he hangs out sometimes. It's a restaurant on the beach. I didn't see him there."

"Anywhere else?"

"Un-uh. I didn't look anywhere else."

"Dan ever get mad? You ever see him get mad at anyone, at his wife or kids?"

"Never. He talked a lot about the kids and brought the kids over...."

"Look, where can we reach you, assuming this warrant thing gets worked out and you catch your plane tomorrow?"

Yesenia gave him the same address in Oregon, Mielke's, that she'd given him before. "I miss my son."

"How long have you known Dan?"

"Around two years."

"How about Trish?"

"She came over to my apartment a couple of times and accused me of sleeping with her husband. I told her I didn't do that. I'm happily married."

"To Abel Rascon, who's in jail?"

"I told her I was teaching him Spanish and she could learn Spanish from me too if she wanted."

"You ever see her any other times?"

"Well, before that happened she came over and talked to me about representing her company, Matol, in Mexico. But after she suspected me of sleeping with her husband, she didn't like me any more."

"When you went to Mexico with Dan those other times, did you sleep with him?"

She looked at Lines as if, after all this, he was guilty of some impropriety. Finally she said, "He gave me some money for `Extra Services.'"

"So you — slept with him?" Lines might have searched for another word here, but he was a churchgoer as well as a cop, and euphemisms are a policeman's best friend. They can mean anything he wants them to later on, when he figures out what spin he wants to give the statement.

"A couple of months after I met him he asked me to go with him to Laughlin. I was real shocked, because I was married to Abel."

"So you didn't go?"

"I told Abel I was going to Sedona to meet Jack, my first husband, and my little boy. Dan rented a plane and we went to Rocky Point. That was the first time I went with Daniel."

Daniel? So there's something almost like reverence at play here. Life is a fucking mystery. "So you had sex that time?"

"Yeah," she smiles. "After all that, I think he was afraid. So I turned him on. I got him so hot, he couldn't control himself."

"How often have you had sex with him over the past two years?"

"About once a week. He's good in bed, I have to admit that."

"When was the last time you had sex with him?"

"In my apartment in Chandler, about three weeks ago."

"Did he talk about not liking it with Trish?"

"No. I'm just younger than her. I'm too tempting. He can't resist."

"Did he ever talk to you about the two of you, you know, just the two of you being alone together in the future."

"No. He knew I was married."

"Does Dan know you're going to Oregon?"

"Uh-huh. To visit Jack. He said not to go and leave him here, but I said I missed my son. But I told him I'm coming back."

"Do you plan to? To keep seeing him?"

She made a face here. "There's no future in it. He's too old for me."

"Have you talked to him about what happened in Rocky Point last week?"

"Yeah, he called like five days ago." She thought about it for a moment, angling her head to advantage. "He said they went to a museum."

Five days before would have been the 28th. The day of Trish's funeral. "What did he tell you about his wife's murder?"

"Nothing. He didn't mention it."

"Did he ever talk to you about hurting her?"

"No. He would never do that."

"Who do you think would?"

She did her thinking thing again. "The mafia."

"The mafia? Why the mafia?"

"One day, when we were in the LA airport, coming back from Cancun, some guy came up to Dan and was talking to him. The guy had a gun."

The guy had a gun. In the airport. "So what does that have to do with the mafia?"

"If Dan was going to have his wife killed, he'd have the Irish mafia do it."

The notorious Green Gumbas, Lines supposed. "Did Dan ever ask you to kill his wife?"

"No. I was on the beach at Manny's the whole time."

"But could you have done it if he asked?"

"No. I walk away from trouble."

"What about your brother?"

"He just drinks too much."

"Well, what about if Trish confronted you, like that time in your apartment when she accused you of sleeping with her husband?"

"Trish is like five-ten and I'm five-four. I would never face Trish."

"Do you know where they were staying?"

"No. You can't find anything around that place. How come you keep asking me this stuff?"

Lines looked at his watch. It was after midnight now, the bewitching hour. "Look, I don't know how to tell you this, but we talked with Dan, and he made you out to be the bad guy."

"When did you talk to him?"

"A while ago."

The ploy seemed too obvious for a minute, but then he could see it working. It always did. "If he thinks that, then you arrest me. I never would think Danny would say that."

"You've told us a lot of lies tonight. That makes you look bad."

"Yeah, but I straightened them out."

Except for one. Out in the hallway, Ruet had shown Lines a social security card bearing the name of Albert Patino that he'd lifted from her purse. Lines showed it to her now.

"It's mine," she said, after a moment. And then she explained about the operation.

"Let's go down to the station and take care of that warrant situation now," Lines said at 12:15. They decided to take her clothes with them, just in case she didn't get back before check-out time the next morning.

Was this charade, at some level, a game of seduction? She never let them go once they'd become involved. She'd still been legally married to Mielke when she'd married Able and then, according to her story, become engaged to Willoughby. They didn't complain, and she didn't hurt any of them on purpose. The way it happened was that Yesenia had her hand tangled in Willoughby's hair. When Lines tugged at her she went without letting go. She told him everything he wanted to hear about what had happened at Rocky Point. And before. Lines told her Dan claimed she'd done the murder. So Dan had done the deed himself, she said. He'd wanted it to be personal, because he despised his wife so much. He had manipulated her into covering it up, as he had bragged about manipulating so many of his employees over the years as a successful manager. He'd promised to marry her....

Yesenia called Dan from the Mesa City jail, and the following morning he paid her bail but refused to see her. Lines found out her fingerprints had been identified in the Las Conchas beach house just a day later. Jack Mielke called later the day she was released; he been waiting for her at the airport in Oregon and wanted to know where the hell she was. Dan told him about the bail but that he didn't know, and didn't want to know, where she was. Dan only spoke to Yesenia one more time, when she called from the car phone of another boyfriend, Harold Goebel, who, Dan later discovered, was driving her to the Mexican border after her family had given her "escape" money. She told Dan she was just calling to say goodbye. Dan told her that was fine; as far as he was concerned, he was finished with her.

Months later, after she was captured, Lines expressed sympathy and offered her a deal. Yesenia would be tried in Mexico, where there was no death penalty, and given immunity in the United States in return for her testimony. She claims she was also promised a TV and other luxuries for her cell and a green card when she got out of the Mexican jail.

After they massaged her testimony, after she sang and cried for them at trial, she was sent back to prison in Mexico with few of her promises fulfilled. Was it that, despite her experience, she didn't know cops and prosecutors? Or was it that she knew them, as she knew all men, and preferred to lie to herself about the depth of their love because those lies gave her life color and drama, and a tragic romance is better than no romance at all?

Siegel

Chapter 14: Conspiracies

Carole always blamed me for nearly missing our daughter's birth. (I had gone out for pizza with her obstetrician, who assured me that Carole couldn't possibly begin delivery for at least another six hours.) Actually, I arrived back at the hospital in plenty of time — with the obstetrician — but I failed to bring enough pizza for the nurses.

"How was I supposed to know that the husband is required to buy pizza for all the OB nurses? It wasn't covered at Lamaze."

"Some things are just a matter of caring," she sobbed. "Of paying attention! Everybody knows you give nurses pizza when your wife's delivering!"

"Oh yeah? Does everybody know what kind?"

That was over eighteen years ago, and I hear about it every other time Carole digs into her tool chest looking for a guilt-wrench. Should I accept this baseless criticism as a fair trade-off for the many other things I could be made to feel guilty for if only she knew about them?

Kinds of guilt is a big issue in the Willoughby case. Legally, criminal guilt is pretty well defined: Dan is guilty of first degree murder if he intended the death of his wife and contributed to it. Intent can be fleeting and momentary: if a tramp on the side of the road gives you the finger and you jump out of your car and beat him to death with your tire iron, you have had plenty of time to "intend" your homicide. If you stop your car and your sadistic cousin gets out and does the job without a word from you, the prosecutor is going to have to prove you intended — or should have known — something like this reasonably could have been expected to happen. "Should have known" is supposed to be a discernable thing, but really it masks the confusion between legal and moral guilt. This is why, to many people, the only distinction between moral and criminal guilt is getting caught. But there are other issues as well. I am guilty about not doing more to feed the poor, for instance, but I cannot be arrested for it, because I have no legal duty to feed them. I am guilty about contemplating adultery, many times in fact. But I do not take steps to accomplish that.

Well, let's say you used to talk to one particular girlfriend at the office, a secretary you've flirted with for years, but with whom you've never actually been sexually intimate. She sends you Valentines each February, you send her chocolate hearts. Her cards are suggestive, but hey, that's twenty-first century Hallmark for you. During the firm Halloween party one year, she comes as Lizzy Borden, complete with an axe dripping red nail polish, and the two of you joke about killing your wife and taking off for Belize together. You were just kidding. Even when the woman later was institutionalized, you didn't seriously entertain the thought that she'd have been confused about that. Then one day she escapes, kills your wife, and comes to you, hospital gown soaked in blood, "Darling, at last we can be together...."

Do you feel guilty? If only you hadn't led her on by flirting, your wife would still be alive. Well, even if Dan is innocent of having actively planned or participated in Trish's murder, a scenario similar to this is the very best he can hope for. How are you going to react when the prosecution emphasizes that he was far more culpable than a flirt, that he had a long-term sexual liaison with Yesenia, and that he had to know she was at least a little nuts? After all, how did Yesenia explain Dan "coincidentally" running into her at Manny's that fatal morning? "He knew how far I could go...."

Dan says, with hindsight, he can see he should have known, but actually had no idea at the time. After all, people have lovers' quarrels, lovers' triangles, affairs and marital disputes, and people rarely get killed. Dan had read, but certainly nothing like this had ever happened in his personal experience.

Technically, this does not amount to legal guilt, but readers tend not to distinguish between legal and moral guilt so readily, and neither do jurors, even when instructed to do so. Furthermore, the prosecution is going to claim that Dan, a skilled salesman and manager, could have knowingly manipulated the psychologically malleable Yesenia into doing the murder even without his direct involvement. If the jury thinks Dan is morally culpable, they may stretch to reach this legal argument.

Somewhere, somehow, one has to deal with the moral implications of Dan's having an affair with this psychopath, of his leading her on to the extent that she believed he wanted her to kill his wife. According to Jack Mielke, over drinks at an airport bar, Dan mentioned going to Mexico with his wife "and coming back without her." Dan denies it, but even if this were true, it may well have been the result of posturing for his girlfriend rather than anything he seriously intended to carry out. Legally such a session might be defused, but the moral implications for Dan would remain.

Some things can't be explained away as macho bullshit. The more difficult problem is tearing apart the prosecution's version of what happened the morning of the murder, when Dan, Yesenia, and Tony met. According to Dan, the meeting was a chance encounter at a familiar hangout where Yesenia would have expected to find him. According to the prosecution, the meeting was prearranged to finalize the details of their plot. The prosecution's embellishment of that meeting between Willoughby and the Patinos is pretty convincing.

Several of Trish's friends testified that she didn't share Dan's enthusiasm for Mexico. Thera, who is not likely to have known, but whose memory seems to have been unfettered by her daughter's death, has testified that Trish would never have gone to Rocky Point had Dan not begged her to. Dan, on the other hand, says that he actually got the idea to rent the beach house there from Thera's son, who had raved about his own getaway vacation in Rocky Point a few months earlier. This is a fact Ochoa might have confirmed, but didn't.

What can Dan have intended if he never actually plotted with Yesenia to murder Trish, yet told her, the morning he met her at Manny's, that he and the kids might be going out alone that afternoon? The prosecution never felt it necessary to consider such a scenario. Their version of events went something like this:

She'd been sitting in the muggy heat of the silver Chevy pickup for what seemed like forever. The sea was only fifty yards away. "What if she goes with them?" she asked herself for the third or fourth time. She'd asked Dan, "How can you be sure she'll stay home if the kids are goin' with you?"

"She hates museums," she reminded herself, waving the joint she'd been smoking like she was painting some kind of picture with it. "'Specially Mexican museums. 'Specially if they're in Mexico. She won't never leave that house if she has a choice."

Yesenia went back to contemplating the half-finished beach house next to the dumpster, wondering how much it cost. Yesenia relit the joint and thought Dan would probably buy it for her when he inherited his wife's money. That wouldn't be so bad.

She heard a door slam and jerked her head back so she could see the front of the beach house. Willoughby and one of the kids, the little boy, went to the driver's side of the Bronco. The older girl got in the front seat with her father, the younger girl in back with the boy.

Yesenia scrunched down in the front seat of the pickup. Besides the black and white polka dot blouse, levis, and black and brown leather boots, she was wearing this stupid black beret and wrap-around sunglasses. Great disguise if you want to look like a criminal and be remembered at the same time. When the Bronco's engine didn't start, she peeked again, saw Dan going back inside, like he forgot something. The kids were staying in the car.

"He's doin' it!" Yesenia squealed with excitement. "He's gonna bash her skull in with that mash, and then, after they go, I'm gonna go in and do her too. And make it look like a robbery."

Yesenia couldn't quite remember the word for what Dan was going to use. It's a thing they used in old times. A big steel ball on a rope. You swing it around on a rope. Danny made it himself.

He could have just bought a hammer, but it had to be special, romantic, Yesenia thought. That's why they were doing it together. It's more romantic that way.

Shit, she thought next, I hope he ain't being too romantic, cause the older girl, Marsha, was going back inside. How long had Dan been in there, anyway? Three minutes? Ten? Should I honk the horn and warn him?

By then the girl was already at the front door, but then it was OK. She couldn't get in. Danny must have locked the door. He'd planned for everything.

Suddenly Danny opened the door from the other side, startling his daughter. He was tucking his shirt into his pants and blocking the door with his body while they talked. What's Mr. I-Got-A-Plan gonna tell the kid if she has to take a leak? But even as she thought it, Yesenia saw Dan had talked himself out of a jam, as usual. In a few seconds, everybody was back in the Bronco and pulling out of short gravel drive. The back door will be open, she told herself confidently, flicking the rest of her joint out the window. Her hand was already on the handle of the pickup's door before the Blazer was out of sight. She couldn't wait to get in there.

At trial, Yesenia testified that Dan committed the bludgeoning himself because he wanted his wife's death to be "personal." She also testified he constructed a mace from materials purchased at an army surplus store, some sort of string and a steel ball. No such weapon was ever found, but the Maricopa County coroner testified Trish's fatal wounds were consistent with this type of weapon, and between them, prosecution and defense attorneys brought into court six or seven different models with which to terrify the jurors.

Yesenia testified to her own entry into the house; Mexican police reported finding tire tracks at the scene, a half-smoked joint in the sand, and the back door unlocked.

The ominous phrases Tony supposedly overheard earlier that morning are refutable. The police probably suggested those to him and he was willing to cooperate to secure his own plea bargain; he probably won't be able to testify to any specific words on the stand. The integrity of Tony's testimony may be further impeached to the extent that he was actually used as a spy by the prosecution, in exchange for leniency; Dan's defense team claims that Tony secretly tape-recorded strategy sessions with David Ochoa, when Ochoa was talking to Tony about being a witness for the defense. But Willoughby meeting Yesenia in Rocky Point certainly isn't good for the case, and there's considerable other evidence of their continuing affair.

Some, though not all of this stuff can be reinterpreted. Dr. Lowry, whose testimony is consistent with the police reports, provides just the kind of damaging detail that fleshes out the prosecution's story. Dan's reluctance to follow the ambulance, his apparent preoccupation with what the police would think, will make him look guilty. But, on the other hand, even if Lowry were right, all this could mean that, while Dan was stunned and horrified by what had happened, he knew instantly that the murder was Yesenia's work, and he had desperately, clumsily attempted to cover it up for that reason....

Has Stevie confiscated Sophie's t-shirt for evidence? Does Carole have it? Is that why she has abandoned me? If Sophie wanted it back, why didn't she ask? I haven't even been sure she was aware I had it, and now wonder, in exquisite detail, if she not only has known all along, but left it on purpose, having more or less planned the events of the previous day. If her nude cockroach dance was staged for some reason other than homage to Isadora Duncan, it might have been because she is tired of Stevie but unable to leave him, she has arranged her own beating and his to bring matters between them to a head. That accomplished, she wants her favorite t-shirt back. *That* she has not grown tired of, although I am history.

Because why else hasn't she come looking for it when I was here, so that, in our mutual, titillatingly coerced confessions, we might spend an hour making love? The obvious answer is that she doesn't want to. Laced with just the right amount of paranoia, this thought will keep me preoccupied for days, until I accept the fact that I was being used, and my usefulness is now over. At the moment, however, I prefer a more elaborate explanation, one that represents how important I must be to her: she wants me to follow her, to follow the trail of the t-shirt, to enter her life as she has entered mine. She knows I like mysteries, drama. I am to track her to her little beach community, where she will confront me (I hope not publicly) with the accusation that I stole her t-shirt, that I am responsible for the turmoil in her life, and I shall have to cajole and plead and make it up to her and fuck her in the warm sand. The t-shirt is my excuse to follow her to her lair.

Of course I don't really believe this. I've tried to explain to Carole that men imagine these things, and even allow them to effect their actions, without for a second really believing such things will happen. Adults don't believe in Santa, yet they decorate their houses with fat men in red suits. Such explanations mostly serve to get me in trouble.

OK, after protesting that I shouldn't have anything to do with her, I'm looking for any lame excuse to see her again. If she hasn't seen the t-shirt, I will have gone there to warn her Carole or Stevie must have it. If Willoughby survives and one day writes my story, I hope he comes up with a better explanation for my behavior than this.

As I set off down the beach in the direction I have seen her go in the past, I think of all the times I've made a fool and a pain in the ass of myself telephoning women who no longer wanted to hear from me, showing up at their work places or apartments and ignoring all the discreet signage reading, "Go Away: Affair Over." Of the time spent knocking, and then listening for the release of held breath, of murmured rustling among the twisted sheets on the other side of the door. Even when I recognize that I truly am better off without these women and have unconsciously wished to be rid of them and to avoid hurting my wife, I can't get beyond the rejection, the disbelief and self-inflicted humiliation. Lust is a busy spider, and we never see the web, only feel the rush of the paralyzing sting.

The glare of mid-afternoon sun off the water makes it impossible to see more than a few hundred yards down the beach. Sighting out of my peripheral vision rather than looking straight on, I am aware of a few beach people gathered near what I imagine to be a tent, but can make out no more than that until I am within thirty yards of them. I have been dangerously wrong on both counts. Two Federales are guarding a sand castle.

Not just any sand castle: this one's five feet high and eight feet in diameter, something the crew who'd built the Cedo might have done over a debauched weekend, except that the monument will last no more than half a day. The Federales are facing inland while the tide rises at their backs, extending and retracting cat-claws of foam, a muscular, threatening pulse edging ever closer to their stuporous prey.

Agustin is squatting on the beach twenty yards away from the Federales, khaki-clad, wearing an outback hat folded up on one side. Something in his demeanor creates his own shade as he smokes a yellowish cigarette, waiting, squinting out across the bay at a large yacht, squinting to protect himself not from the sun, as I am, but from seeing too much, as if his gaze, resigned though not easily subdued, might overload his sensitive detective's brain with too much information. The Federales are pretending not to look at me, but clearly intend to intimidate me with their automatic weapons and stone cold attitudes, to forbid my passage by their mere presence. They win this game hands down. I feel obligated to gesture toward Agustin, as if I have come to meet with him.

He gives me a pleasant smile, and I attempt to ask him if he has seen a tall blond girl wearing a black t-shirt, colors, clothing, and body parts being easy enough to point to. He nods and points out toward the yacht. I hadn't really expected an answer, and have been covertly sniffing for traces of fried chicken. "Whose?" I ask, following his yacht-bound finger with my own. I know the word is "Que-something," but again I get by.

"Sr. Brown." His eyes narrow a little more, and I understand that they are all here, Agustin and the Federales, because of Sr. Brown. Agustin shifts his body slightly as he stubs out the cigarette in the sand, his fourth or fifth, and I notice for the first time he is wearing a big .38 on his waist, like an old-fashioned gunslinger, an eye-catching addition to his chicken shack wardrobe. He notices me noticing, smiles sourly, gesturing toward the boat again, and says, "Safe passage."

The Federales don't like it when he gestures toward the boat. Maybe it is their boat to gesture toward. Just as assiduously as they have ignored my presence, so do they seem to over-react to Agustin's every move. Agustin must be watching them, too, out of the corner of his eye, because, when his hand goes toward his gun, and their automatic rifles come suddenly off their shoulders, and he then offers me a cigarette from the crumpled pack he's pulled from his gunbelt before the Federales can round on us, and the Federales suddenly pretend they are only making themselves more comfortable or performing that barrel maintenance they've been planning on getting to for some time. Agustin's bloodshot brown slits of eyes sparkle and a thin smile travels across his lips and disappears with the tide.

Although I don't smoke, I accept the cigarette and look more closely at the sand castle. If both sides here are guarding it from each other, everybody is going to be out of a job come high tide. This is a shame, because it's a pretty impressive piece of work. Carole would photograph it from six angles if she were here, and I could make up a story to tell everybody, the possibility of her complicity with my lies spicing the evening's entertainment for both of us. She never would let on, even to me, what she actually remembered and what she knew I was making up.... The story about this one would be that a famous sculptor (I'd have to research a likely candidate who traveled around the world's beaches) always modeled his works in sand before he went to more permanent materials, simply leaving the evidence to be destroyed by the elements. Then one day his wife seemed to die of some tropical fever; only the sculptor knew her death was actually the result of a blowfish poison meant for him, left in revenge because he had seduced the wife of a local fisherman. The artist stopped producing works, as far as the world knew, but still wandered the beaches, building in sand, building for the day only....

He would have to be a cubist, I thought. This particular castle looked nothing like the Excaliber in Vegas.

But that story is too unrelated to what I actually see here. A more relevant story, I now surmise, is about Sr. B, a millionaire criminal with connections everywhere in the Americas. He is also a famous romancer, whose lovers, even though he may have met them only once, patiently await his call, whether it be for months or years. Sporadically, but with the emotional accuracy of Cupid turned Robin Hood, he assures that each of them receives gifts, delivered by children or wandering vagrants or, most often, by unseen messengers, the gifts left on window sills, under pillows, tucked among a basket of clean laundry waiting to be hung. These gifts are sometimes valuable and sometimes whimsically intimate, to show he has not forgotten them either, although there be no other communication. When Sr. B is to meet a lover, one of these amazing sand castles appears on the beach to signal the woman. On her early morning rounds to the market, on her way to work, looking out her kitchen window beyond where her children of peculiarly mixed features are playing on the shore, the lover will perceive the signal within a few moments of its mysterious appearance, will make excuses, arrangements, apologies, and excuse herself for a private stroll down the beach toward the sand castle, where a launch awaits....

So that would be Sophie, in this case. But what of Agustin's role in this? Is he her jealous husband (God knows who she's married to today, if anyone) or surrogate father, come to kill the wealthy despoiler? I try to imagine Agustin's reaction when, through Frenchy, he is asked this question. He notices my attention, and says to me, "No blood."

"No blood?"

"No blood on walls." He means at the Willoughby crime scene, of course. Well, this is a major blow to my defense. My best argument, I'd thought, would be the complete lack of physical evidence tying Dan to the crime. No blood on his clothing following such a brutal and messy murder would have made good sense to a jury. But now I'm being told the killer had managed to bash in Trish's head without spattering blood on anything. This is a real pisser.

"Sophia?" I say, gesturing toward the yacht.

"OK," he says, nodding in that direction, then shrugging. What the hell does that mean, other than he and I aren't going to jump the Federales, leap onto a jet ski buried in the sand castle, and storm the yacht to rescue Sophie from the probably welcome attentions of Sr. B? It means, with this migraine-inducing glare reflecting directly into my eyes from the barrels of submachine guns, that, as soon as I finish his cigarette, I shake hands with Agustin and head back up the beach in the direction I've come.

I'm a slow thinker, all my life a half step behind myself. But even I can see the fork in my immediate future: I can either trash everything I've ever created for a brief fling with a possibly psychotic child, or I can decide never to see her again, return to the United States of Mental Health and Responsible Living and at least try to tie together the torn strands of the lives I've left dangling there. (As an attorney, I've learned that the phrasing of the question determines the answer.)

At the moment, I decide I have been taking an innocent walk along the beach and that it is my wife's behavior that should concern the karmic referees. After all, despite my guilty thoughts, I haven't actually done anything wrong. It wasn't my fault Sophie left her t-shirt in my room. I didn't plan to get in a fist fight with her husband, and, when I did, I merely defended myself. How could I have foreseen she was going to stomp him while I was trying to get the sand out of my eyes? I didn't have sex with her by any post-Carter presidential definition. Why shouldn't I just find Carole, apologize for ignoring her – and then ask where the hell she's been for the past twenty-four hours?

I can still be lucky – at least luckier than Dan Willoughby was. I can get out of this without permanent damage.

Siegel

Chapter 15: Somebody Else's Saint

Dan Willoughby stood in the doorway of his vacation home, watching the ambulance pulling out of the driveway, the police cars pulling in. His children were huddled behind him around the heatless hearth, vacant and numb as delicate, prehistoric mummies frozen in a glacier.

This is not the fresco of a saint Dr. Lowry has drawn.

When you know evidence that's bad for your client is likely to come out at trial, the usual strategy is to broach it yourself with your client on direct examination. Then, instead of having a client whom the defense has exposed as a terrible sonofabitch anxious to hide his weaknesses, you have an essentially honest client, with human weaknesses, sure, but one who will be the first to admit them. You then hope the jury will believe your client would also admit any other bad allegations if in fact these really were true, and, instead of believing the defense, they will rely on the rest of your client's denial.

One such part of the Willoughby case concerns the first conversation Dan had with Kay Lines shortly after it became obvious the police were going to be looking at him as a suspect.

That Dan would be a suspect must have been apparent from his reception by the Huishes upon his return to Arizona. Arriving at their house a few days after Trish's death, expecting to share sympathies, grieving husband to grieving family, Dan was brutally rebuffed. Instead of embraces, there were only accusations. Thera Huish flatly told Dan that she didn't care what the evidence was or whom the police were looking for, she was convinced he had murdered her daughter.

It is common for grieving people to strike out at whoever happens to be handy, but this seemed pretty excessive even for a mother-in-law. And it did not stop there. Thera had already been on the phone to Kay Lines, whom she knew from her Church Stake. Apparently within two days of the murder, well before any information from Mexico was available to her, she told Lines she was sure Dan was responsible. Most professional investigators would have taken what Thera had to say with a grain of salt. Most would have tried to calm her, at least telling her she ought to wait upon the evidence before rushing to any conclusions.

Technically, neither Lines or the AG's office had any business being involved in the Willoughby case early on. Trish's murder had occurred in Mexico, and there could not have been any hard evidence at that point giving Arizona jurisdiction. Additionally, if Willoughby had been suspected of having plotted his wife's murder, the investigation would have proceeded through the local police force developing that evidence, perhaps in Gilbert, where the Willoughbys lived, or in nearby Chandler, where Yesenia's apartment was. Despite these procedural peculiarities, the Gilbert Police Department was persuaded to accept the AG's "assistance" and then immediately remanded to a secondary position.

Acting without the approval of a supervisor, Lines interviewed Willoughby on March 1, 1991, a couple days after his return to the United States. Perhaps because Dan was a lapsed Mormon and Lines a Stake officer, Lines immediately attacked Dan not about the crime but about his immorality. In a panic, Dan denied having had any extra-marital affairs, although he was well aware that everyone around him knew of his relationship with Yesenia.

The appearance of Kay Lines as Thera Huish's co-conspirator, Dan says, panicked him totally. He knew Thera wanted the money from T&T Enterprises. (If you believe Thera herself, rather than Dan, Dan knew she also wanted to secure the million dollars in insurance coverage from the business.) Dan knew that a man who kills his wife cannot profit by the crime through inheritance, so Thera could be counted on to tag him as the murderer. Thera knew Dan had had an affair with Yesenia, so there was no doubt in Dan's mind that Lines would be pursuing Yesenia to implicate him.

Dan's lie about his association with Yesenia might be damaging, but a decent lawyer would seek to "draw the sting" of such evidence by asking Dan on direct exam, "Did you lie to Kay Lines about having had an affair with Yesenia Patino?"

"Yes."

"Didn't you know it was wrong to give false information to a police investigator?"

"Yes. I admit I did the wrong thing. I just panicked."

"Why would you do a thing like that?"

"I was afraid."

"Why would an innocent man be afraid, Dan?"

"Because I was being railroaded by Lines and Huish. Yesenia's not very bright, and I knew he'd threaten her and make her say things that weren't true —"

Prosecution: "Objection! The witness is speculating! The answer is not responsive and the prosecution moves it be stricken —"

"Your Honor —"

Judge: "Will counsel approach the bench?"

If this isn't done, it's not hard to imagine a juror's skepticism about Willoughby's behavior. But at trial, Willoughby's attorney not only never allowed him to take the stand to present his excuse, he never presented the argument that Dan HADN'T been involved in the escape.

In fact, by the time he interviewed Dan, Lines already had Gilbert police staking out Yesenia's apartment in Chandler, and interviewed her at the Airport Hilton two days later. After her protracted charade and admission that she and Tony had been in Rocky Point on the day of the murder, Lines got in touch with the police in Rocky Point. By the following day, Mexican investigators had confirmed that Yesenia's fingerprints were inside the beach house.

Dan denies planning Yesenia's disappearance, or giving her money to hide from the police with her husband, Jack Mielke. Since their separation, Yesenia had remained on good terms with Mielke, who literally had made a woman out of her by giving her the money for her sex-change surgery back in 1984. Mielke, in turn, appeared to accept his wife's latest lover. The three had met on several occasions, swapping drinks and stories in airport bars. While Mielke's relationship with Yesenia had always been stormy, they remained tied to each other by their long and complicated history and by their son Charlie. Because Mielke had driven down from Eugene, Oregon, to cart away most of Yesenia's belongings in October 1990, Dan says he failed to connect Yesenia's plan to fly back to Oregon in March 1991 with the murder. This was simply Yesenia's long-awaited final departure.

Likewise, Dan denies having anything to do with her "getaway." It was another of Yesenia's boyfriends, a Harold Goebel, who took her to her mother in Chandler, and Yesenia's mother and brothers gave her a little over $300 and drove her to the Nogales border, from where she made her way to the family home in Mexico. Dan says all he knew was that Yesenia had been planning, long before the murder, to rejoin Jack Mielke and their son Charlie. The "missing" testimony of Lona Mason, that she saw Yesenia with Mielke after her disappearance and before the police announced her as a fugitive, might contribute to proving Dan's assertion.

Because Lines had no proof of Yesenia's direct involvement the night he picked her up at the airport hotel, he had to let her go on bail the next day. She had disappeared by the time her fingerprints were confirmed on the knives protruding from Trish's head and on a bloody coke bottle in the kitchen where she had paused for refreshment. ("Jamming those knives in there was such hard work," she is reported to have complained. "They kept bending and slipping. I nearly cut myself.")

On April 26, however, Lines arrested Tony Patino and charged him with conspiracy to commit murder. He was released on his own recognizance after two weeks, when Lines was assured of his full cooperation against Willoughby. No one ever has questioned the AG's Office about what evidence they had against him in the first place.

Police put Yesenia's photo on billboards and buses for months in various locations in Mexico while they were looking for her. She must have loved the celebrity. She was probably still bragging about it when, around midnight on the 6th of December 1991, she was arrested at a well known tourist haunt in Mazatlan called Senor Frogs. Lines and prosecutor Steve Mitchell had gone down there on a tip and County money, but were just about to hang it up when Lines recognized a peculiarly raucous laugh he'd last heard at the airport hotel.

Dan was arrested in Gilbert on December 9, 1991. Through his attorney, David Ochoa, Dan had arranged to give himself up at the Gilbert police station at any time any agency suggested they wanted to arrest him. When that day came, however, he was jumped on the pavement in front of his house by six burly cops, hand-cuffed, and dragged stunned to the station house, where he listened for some time in disbelief to the Gilbert police and the

AG's investigators argue over which of them was to get the official credit for his "collar."

At trial, Dan's imaginary friend Jack Mielke recalled that, over drinks at the airport, Dan had mentioned going to Mexico with his wife and coming back alone. Dan claims the prosecution got Mielke to lie by threatening to deport his son. Outsiders must speculate that, among other things, Jack may still have been protecting the love of his life, Albert Yesenia Patino Victoria Mielke. Ochoa raised no arguments when the prosecution presented Mielke as an objective witness with no on-going ties to Yesenia.

So I am prepared to draw the sting of anything Carole may have heard about my behavior over the past few days. But first I ask Frenchy if he's seen the big yacht that's dominated the harbor for the past few days.

"Sr. Brown's boat? He took his son and daughter-in-law and left," Frenchy says absently.

"His son?" I manage.

"Stephano. Not the nicest kid you ever met. Likes to hang out on Sandy Beach to impress the gringo girl's with his daddy's big boat."

"Where'd they go?"

"Who knows? But the season's almost over, so I don't think they'll be back soon."

"And that Sophie? She was the son's wife?"

"Wife, girlfriend, I don't know. But they fight a lot, so they're probably married."

Some confessions are best kept to the last moment, because they may never be needed. This is one reason why many defendants never testify at all.

Chapter 16: Murderer

Yesenia and Dan found each other at Manny's the morning of the murder. Having confirmed his worst fear, though, that she'd taken money from the rent account and come down here to buy drugs with it, he didn't know what to do with her. He told her his family was waiting back at the beach house, that he had just come by to make sure she was OK.

"I want to have a drink with you," she said.

"Manny's isn't serving. It's some kind of holiday. I just don't have the time."

"I want to have a drink with you, Danny," she whined, pressing his arm against her body. "We can go somewhere else. Vina del Mar, they got wine and beer."

"I can't, Chiquita —"

But she pleaded with him with such intensity that he finally agreed to have just one, and followed her and Tony in his pickup the short distance to the other restaurant in his Bronco. Dan stuck to his guns there. What was the point of bringing his family all the way down here for a reconciliation with Trish just to abandon her for an afternoon fuck with Yesenia? And Yesenia still had the five hundred bucks, for chrissake. Or at least she said she did.

After Dan left her in the Vina del Mar, Yesenia had a second beer and thought. It was time. She was tired of waiting for Dan to make a choice. She had come down here to make something happen. She shouldered the enormous purse and told Tony she was going to the little girls' room.

It was a good bathroom, one where you could lock the door and keep everybody out of your business. She pulled a bottle of purified water and a blackened spoon out of the purse, and a tiny piece of cotton. She put a few drops of water in the spoon, and used the cotton to mix in her dose of cocaine. Tying off her arm with a red ribbon, she filled a syringe with the mixture from the spoon and shot it into a vein on the inside of her arm.

She'd done this before. She didn't shoot it all the time, because Dan disapproved of drugs, wouldn't even snort with her, but shooting coke was her favorite rush. Today, though, she had prepared for something different. She had to be steady and calm today. She took the dose of heroin from her purse and crushed it with the spoon, the way El Negro had told her. Then she repeated the process with the water, the cotton, the syringe. She had never shot heroin before, but it cost the same as the coke, fifty dollars, and somehow this reassured her. If fifty dollars worth of coke wouldn't kill you, fifty dollars worth of heroin couldn't either.

It felt pretty damn good. She washed off her arm, and rolled down her sleeve. The fix kit rattled a little against the heavy thing inside her purse, even though that was wrapped in the ski mask. "Okay. Time to go," she told the face in the mirror. "Time to go," she told Tony back at the table.

"Where we going?"

"I have to collect some money for Dan." Tony looked worried. "It's OK. He'll be watching us."

The speedball was really working great. Out at the truck, she asked Tony for the keys.

"But, Sis, it's a standard. You don't drive a standard."

"I don't care, Tony. We're in Mexico. Here it doesn't matter if you're struggling to get there. All that matters is to get where you're going."

Tony acquiesced more easily than the truck, which stalled out every other time she used the clutch. But when she was sure she could get by on her own, she dropped Tony on a street corner.

"You're going to wait here while I go and collect the money."

"You going to be all right?" he asked.

"Don't worry. I'll collect the money and be right back. Dan's going to be watching me. Everything will be fine."

He nodded and she pulled away. Lurching onto the dirt road near the house in Las Conchas, she parked on the sandy street about a block away from the front door. The two younger kids were playing outside. She pulled the black wool ski mask on over her face and slid down in the seat so no one would see her.

By the time Dan came out, she might have been waiting an hour or only five minutes. Her mouth had gotten a little dry, so she'd opened a Diet Coke. The heroin had her so relaxed she wasn't sure and didn't care how long she'd been waiting. Somehow Marsha and the kids already had gotten into the Bronco parked in the driveway. Yesenia was sure she'd been watching; how had she missed that?

As soon as they were gone, she started the truck and managed to jerk it around to the back of the house. When it died, it was about three-quarters hidden by the new construction. That would have to do.

She knew it would. She felt great, loose and comfortable. Smiling as if she did this every day, she reached into the black purse for its final secret. The black metal ball the size of her fist was hooked to a chain. It had seemed like a good idea the night she had her friend steal it for her off the wall of the El Capri. Not as good as a gun with a silencer, maybe, but more personal, more appropriate for personal business.

She crept up on the back of the house. On the arid little patio, she picked up the big, bent nail that El Negro had showed her how to use to flip up the little hook that held the screen door shut, smiling to herself at how easy it was. Without thinking about it, she put the nail back down and picked up the Diet Coke again. Carefully she pushed the door open and slid through.

Danny and the kids could come back at any minute, she thought. What would they do? Would he help her kill Trish? Would he stop her? Would he turn her over to the police? Would he hurt Yesenia for trying to hurt his wife, take the mace out of her hand and beat her with it? If Trish saw her there, would she finally realize how determined Yesenia was and simply give Dan up to her?

All Yesenia knew for certain was that a bomb was about to explode in their lives. She moved into the room. The fuse was lit.

Trish was lying on the bed right in front of her, one of those Matol magazines stuck in front of her face. Yesenia was thinking maybe she would sell that crap when she became Danny's wife, somebody would have to take over, after all — when Trish sensed someone else was in the room. Trish looked up and saw her husband's crazy lover standing next to the bed wearing a ski mask and carrying a Diet Coke, something else in her other hand.

Trish was a head taller than Yesenia and in pretty good shape, but before she could rise off the bed, Yesenia wound up with the mace and swung it sideways with all her might at Trish's head. The blow knocked the bigger woman straight back into the bed. Blood sprayed onto the mattress and the wall behind her. She seemed unconscious. Yesenia hit her again and again, now swinging the mace from behind her head, using all her force. A terrific sense of power flooded her. At last it was happening.

After she had hit her about six times, Yesenia was pretty sure she was dead. Yesenia covered the battered head with the bed sheets. But what if she wasn't dead? Wait, she was still breathing! Damn. Yesenia went into the kitchen to look for a knife, but all she could find were these little knives, not much better than butter knives. She put the Diet Coke down and rummaged through the drawers, but couldn't find anything better. She took all the knives she could find back into the bed room, and started to stab Trish in the head with them, right through the bed sheet. And then in the chest and the stomach and the body. They barely seemed to leave a mark. Finally Yesenia gave up on the knives and brought a nylon cord out of her pocket, a nylon cord she'd had Dan buy her at the Navy Surplus store. She'd told him she was going to make a braid out of it, but even then she must have known, and maybe he had too, because he'd given her that funny look. Now it would be his contribution to this execution. But when she got on top of Trish and tried to wrap the nylon cord around Trish's neck to strangle her, the bed was too soft. It kept shifting out from under her. Yesenia couldn't get her balance, and the cord was too short.

Trish was still breathing. Yesenia gave up. I've got to take some things, make it look like a robbery, and get out of here, she thought. She found the rings on the dresser, and took the only cash she could see, about thirteen dollars.

And then she left.

That's pretty much what Yesenia told us happened in her most recent confession, under oath and in front of a video cam in Caborca Prison in 1997. Kay Lines and Steve Mitchell were in attendance, as was the Appellate

Prosecutor Paul McMurdy, so Yesenia can't be accused of pandering to her audience. But, ...

One of attorney Ochoa's biggest blunders seems to have been his handling of Yesenia's brother, Tony Patino. Not only did Ochoa apparently confide in Tony, who was actually working for the prosecution, but he failed to impeach Tony's damaging testimony at trial by pointing out that he was testifying in exchange for immunity from prosecution for the murder for which he initially had been charged. By law, the prosecution must have had sufficient evidence against him to believe he was the real, or one of the real, murderers, yet the jury was never told what that evidence was. (Nor were jurors told that Patino had been denied counsel and his Miranda rights violated when he was first arrested and questioned, although Ochoa had complained about this at a prior hearing.) The prosection would have been doubly embarrassed, since they denied at trial that evidence implicating anyone but Dan and Yesenia even existed. The gate guard at Las Conchas claimed to have seen a grey pickup like Tony's leaving the area after the murder with *several* people in it. Not only does this place Tony at the scene and further discredit Yesenia's "confession" at trial that she and Dan did the murder together, but it should have shown the jury that the state was playing games when they denied there was any evidence that any witness at the scene had seen the "dark colored pickup" Dan insisted had been reported to him.

Yet, without even examining that evidence himself, David Ochoa announced to the jury that ultimately convicted Dan that Tony Patino must indeed be innocent! It is not hard to envision a somewhat different scenario:

"Okay. Time to go," Yesenia told the face in the mirror. "Time to go," she told Tony back at the table.

"Where we going?"

"I have to collect some money for Dan." Tony snorted. *"It's OK. He'll be watching us."*

The speedball was really working great. Out at the truck, she asked Tony for the keys.

"You don't drive a standard."

"It's OK."

"Like hell. You ain't wrecking my transmission. I'll drive."

Yesenia directed him to Las Conchas. Tony gave her an earful about the fucking rich gringo bastards who owned all these vacation houses, and she realized he'd had more than a couple beers at Manny's. Drink made him mean, but, instead of feeling worried about that, she had an idea. Fumbling in the big shoulder bag on the floor of the pickup, she couldn't help smiling to herself.

"What the hell is that thing?"

Yesenia unwound the cord around the big steel ball and then dangled it between her hands like a yoyo. *"It's a mace. Knights of the Round Table used it to bash each other in the head."*

"Like hell. Didn't I see that hanging on the wall over at El Capri?"

"That don't mean it's not a real weapon." She swung it just a little in the confines of the cab, causing Tony to swerve and swear at her.

"Cut that shit out." He pulled to a halt behind a big construction dumpster where the gringos were gouging out yet another insult to the Mexican people. Yesenia popped out of the cab and snuck around the back of the dumpster. Tony heard a metallic clang. *"What the hell are you doing?"* He got out in disgust and found her flailing at the sand with the mace. She nearly caught him with a back swing, and he grabbed at her wrist and pried it away from her.

"Owww. You hurt my wrist."

"I hurt your wrist? You're lucky you didn't kill yourself with this thing." For emphasis, he swung the mace in a wide arc — and snapped the top off a two-by-four that had been protruding from the dumpster. Christ. This thing was dangerous.

"Oh, you're so good with that!" Yesenia squealed. *"Let me try."* She clunked it feebly into the side of the dumpster a couple of times, missing the two-by-four by at least a foot.

"Exactly what are you hoping to hit with that?" Tony asked finally.

"Dan's wife," she said, matter-of-factly. *"With her out of the way, he'll marry me in a minute."*

"You're still married to Rascon."

"He's in jail. He don't care. There'll be plenty of money to go around for everyone when I'm Mrs. Dan Willoughby. Her business is worth millions, you know."

Millions? Tony thought. Finally he snorted and took the mace back from her. *"You better let me do this, Mrs. Willoughby. You might break a fucking nail."*

Yesenia steadfastly has refused to implicate her brother. There appears no more physical evidence against him than against Dan Willoughby, but, if reports are true that there was at least one other person in the pickup truck that fled the scene, who could Yesenia be protecting besides her brother? At the very least, an argument fashioned on this scenario might have interested jurors who believed Yesenia herself lacked the physical strength to kill Trish.

Chapter 17: Ineffective Assistance

When Yesenia disappeared from the airport hotel, she went not to Portland, to the now exposed Mielke, but to Mexico, to Valle Hermosa in Taumalipas, where her mother, although also living in Chandler, still maintained the family house. How do you imagine the mother who gave birth to Yesenia? Like Grendel's mother, does she embrace the transsexual murderer as fruit of her loins? Which bothers this good Catholic the most, that her son has become a daughter, or that the daughter has proven to be a cold blooded killer?

"What are you doing here?" her mother hisses. "The police in Phoenix and in Mexico are looking for you. Do you want the police coming here, and arresting me, and taking me from my home?"

"Gee, hi, Mamma. Nice to see you too, Mamma."

"Your brother Tony is in prison in Phoenix because of you, because he knows something about the murder." Tony is her favorite, although, in fact, she knows he is a nasty drunk. Even his mother suspects he is capable of just about anything when he's drunk, or at least anything a five-foot six inch man can do behind his opponent's back.

But Yesenia is devoted to him. Tearfully, Yesenia agrees to give herself up in order to free her brother. Then she flees to the hills, then back to the tourist towns along the coast. At bad moments, when she can't help thinking that she is delaying on her promise to her mother, she says to herself with a little grin, Tony can screw himself; the moron used to laugh whenever he said that to her: "Albert, he's the only boy I know who really can screw himself."

But in the house in Las Conchas, she had needed him... .

Then Kay Lines and the Mexican police arrested Yesenia in Mazatlan. They interviewed her for about four hours in the Mazatlan police station. Her interview was a series of denials and partial contradictions, but, surprisingly, they didn't seem to press her, at least not where she was the weakest. She couldn't figure it out. Lines had tied her up in knots so easily back at the airport hotel. And then, as she was being led back to her cell, Lines said to her, "Yesenia, don't be afraid. Don't be afraid to tell us, because we know Dan Willoughby killed his wife." She looked at him and didn't respond, but, after thinking about it for a moment, she understood.

They moved her to Hermosillo and then to Caborca, and kept after her the whole time. They reminded her about the death penalty in the United States. Finally, she agreed to testify that Dan and she had planned the murder in the United States, and that Dan had been the one to crush his wife's skull with a mace. She said she would swear it had been his idea, if they would let Tony go free and promise not to prosecute her in the US, and if Lines would give her back the "engagement ring" Dan had bought her.

And then the trial came, and finally the day she was to testify against Dan. They brought her into an anteroom just off the courtroom, and, through the door, she saw Dan sitting at the defendants' table with his attorney and investigator. The jury was listening to the judge tell them not to be influenced by what had happened to Rodney King in LA that summer. She only saw Dan's back, but she couldn't do it. At the last minute, she couldn't do it. She told the prosecutor, Steve Mitchell, she couldn't do it.

He stared at her for a minute and walked away, and then one of his people came, Debbie Schwartz.

"Yesenia, it's your life or his," Debbie reminded her. "Not to mention Tony's. We'd rather have Willoughby."

"I can't do it. I can't testify against Dan Willoughby."

"Then I guess it will be your life."

"It can't be me either," she cried. "I'm too afraid."

Debbie sat her down on the long wooden bench outside the courtroom, then got up to get Yesenia a glass of water. When she came back, she handed Yesenia a long white pill with the water. "Take this. It'll make you feel better."

And it did too. Not so loose and confident as the heroin she'd taken on the day of the murder, but stronger and full of energy again. She dried her eyes and by the time she was called to testify, she felt it was time to get on with her life. It was time to make things happen.

The AG's Office denies giving Yesenia any sort of medication before her trial testimony, and Dan denies giving her an engagement ring. (He did give her a ring, but, as he points out, she was already married to two other men!) In any event, this is what Yesenia Patino swore to under oath when she was deposed in her jail cell on February 24, 1997, in Nogales, Sonora, in front of Kay Lines, Steve Mitchell, and several other people from both sides. When a small part of it finally was shown on TV news nearly three years later, it made a brief if sensational splash. But it didn't win Dan a right to a new trial, where it might be heard.

In 1995, when the Arizona Supreme Court reviewed his conviction, Dan argued that the state had no power to try him for a murder committed in Mexico; the Supreme Court found that, although the fatal blow had been struck in Mexico, there was sufficient evidence that premeditation for the crime had occurred in Arizona to give the state jurisdiction. Willoughby argued that the state didn't have probable cause (sufficiently reasonable belief) to try him for conspiracy; the Court said that the conversations testified to by Yesenia and Jack Mielke provided plenty of circumstantial evidence of conspiracy. Willoughby argued that the state could not impose the death penalty for a murder committed in Mexico, a jurisdiction without the death penalty; the Court said that Arizona could invoke its own penalties in its own courtroom, and that this act did not violate the extradition treaty between the United States and Mexico prohibiting the death penalty in such cases because Mexico had not invoked the treaty. The Court said there was sufficient evidence to support the jury's verdict on all counts, that excusing jurors who said they could not convict someone who might get the death penalty was constitutional, and that, because Ochoa had failed to object to various prosecution tactics at trial, those could not be appealed now.

Two years later Dan Willoughby came to court on his very last chance of saving his life. He had a post-trial hearing in which he argued he was entitled to a new trial because his attorney had done such a poor job of representing him. The logic behind such a claim is that a person who goes to court without reasonable legal representation has been deprived of his constitutional right to a fair trial. Tom Thinnes, a highly respected, veteran trial lawyer and Willoughby's expert witness, testified that this was the worst case of ineffective assistance of counsel that he'd ever heard of, much less seen, in over thirty years of practice. Thinnes cited dozens of errors Dan's trial attorney, David Ochoa, had made, from the imaginary and lethal opening statement, to his failure to object to repeated unfair and inadmissible remarks introduced by the prosecution and its witnesses. Ochoa himself never even interviewed such potential witnesses as the insurance agents who sold Trish her policies and the Mexican pathologist who found the cause of Trish's death to be the stab wounds Yesenia inflicted; he failed to call such witnesses as any of the six people who reported seeing the mysterious dark truck leaving Las Conchas; most amazingly, he never used any of the three tapes in which Yesenia admitted she alone had planned and executed the murder — even when cross-examining her after she testified Dan had planned and committed the murder! Any one of these blunders, Thinnes opined, might have been fatal to this case.

"But Mr. Thinnes," Judge Howe noted, "we can't hold every attorney up to your high standard. What the Court needs to know is if Mr. Ochoa's representation might have been adequate by the average standard in this legal community."

"Your Honor," Thinnes replied, "a first year law student could have done a better job in defending Mr. Willoughby."

Indeed, when Ochoa himself took the stand, Judge Howe asked the attorney, recently returned from a sabbatical selling real estate, "Mr. Ochoa, do you remember me calling you into chambers after your opening statement in this case?"

"Yes, Your Honor."

"You had just argued that your own client had never intended to murder his wife, only to extort money from her, and that she accidentally had been killed in the process. Do you recall that?"

"Yes, Your Honor."

"And I pointed out to you that you had just told the jury your client was guilty of felony murder for profit, itself a capital offense."

"Yes, Your Honor. I hadn't thought it out all the way."

"Where did that line of argument come from, Mr. Ochoa?"

We were holding our breath here. Everybody involved in the trial knows Ochoa was incompetent, but the fear in

Dan's camp was that Ochoa would try to save his own skin — clearly jeopardized by sanctions from the state bar and possibly a hefty malpractice claim — by lying to the Court and saying he was just repeating what Dan told him. If Ochoa chose to say that Dan confessed his guilt in private, with no other witnesses around, no one could disprove it, and Dan would be executed.

"Your Honor, I made it up. I got the idea from a focus group we were in, and I'd been thinking about it, but I didn't decide to say that until the trial started."

"Dan Willoughby never told you that?"

"No, Your Honor. We never even discussed it."

There was a gasp of relief from Dan's corner. Ochoa might not be much of an attorney, but he was an honorable man, willing to fall on his sword for what he'd done to his client.

Judge Howe knew all this instantly, and he couldn't help smiling a bit. "Mr. Ochoa, when we had that conversation after opening statements, do you think I should have declared a mistrial right then?"

"Well, Your Yonor," Ochoa replied, uncomfortable at being put in the position of judging the judge, "can I speak truthfully?"

"Why not? You're not the President."

"Yes, sir. You should have kicked me out."

Faced with this testimony that Ochoa's incompetence had put Dan on death row, the prosecution began to argue that Ochoa hadn't done that bad a job considering the position they'd put him in. I'd never seen this tactic before in a courtroom; essentially the prosecution said that they were so devious, Ochoa did as good a job as could have been expected, so Willoughby shouldn't get a new trial. But they were hamstrung in this approach by needing to avoid sanctions on their side. As Judge Howe reminded Paul McMurdy, the prosecution's skillful appellate advocate, he could grant a new trial for prosecutorial misconduct as well as for defense incompetence.

What emerged was half a scandal. The prosecution actually claimed that it was able to anticipate Ochoa's defense because it obtained tape recordings of Ochoa discussing defense strategy with a number of witnesses, particularly Tony Patino. The AG originally charged Tony with first degree murder and conspiracy to commit murder, only to drop those charges in exchange for his "cooperation," which apparently included wearing a wire every time he went into Ochoa's office. In a fabulous display of legal contortionism, McMurdy first argued the prosecution was entitled to do this, because they distrusted Ochoa after he allegedly requested Patino attempt to record conversations for him with his own family members. But when it came to answering questions about who authorized such a procedure, McMurdy denied that anyone on the AG's staff did anything wrong. Even though Investigator Debbie Schwartz's initials are all over those Special Investigative Reports, she testified she has no recollection of ever having seen them, much less of authorizing them.

Eventually, Judge Howe took over Schwartz's cross-examination himself.

"You're telling the Court, Ms. Schwartz, that you don't recall if Tony Patino was your confidential informant?"

"No, Your Honor, I don't recall."

"Do you know why the report was prepared?"

"I have no recollection of that."

"Did you do anything else to investigate Mr. Ochoa?"

"I don't recall."

"Did Investigator Lines?"

"I don't recall."

"Did Mr. Mitchell?"

"I just don't recall anything about that aspect of this case."

Schwartz did admit that Yesenia called her several times to tell her that she was going to change her testimony to admit she was the one who committed the murder, but Schwartz "doesn't recall" if any of those calls were ever disclosed to the defense. She recalled that she and Lines went down to Caborca prison to convince Yesenia to testify that Dan had committed the murder — but she didn't remember what was said. Finally, after prodding from the judge, she admitted that they "probably" threatened to prosecute Yesenia and her brother Tony in Arizona if she attempted to recant.

Finally, McMurdy suggested that Ochoa himself may have made the tapes and voluntarily turned them over to the prosecution. Because Ochoa was no longer in Court, he couldn't be examined on this issue.

"But why would he do that?" Judge Howe wanted to know.

"Because he had been warned by the Court not to tamper with witnesses."

Early in the case, Ochoa had accused the prosecution of "losing" witness interviews and misrepresenting testimony from other interviews by editing witness remarks. The prosecution responded that Ochoa was suborning perjury by suggesting testimony to Yesenia's family — and threatened to file charges against Ochoa himself for this offense. Thus, Ochoa spent the rest of the trial under the fear that, if he attempted too vigorous of a defense, he himself would be the next defendant. To prevent his own indictment, therefore, he agreed to a completely one-sided arrangement that he would not interview a single witness unless the prosecution was present at the interview. Additionally, McMurdy now theorized, Ochoa probably had wired Patino himself in order to prove his compliance by taping his own conversations.

But Judge Howe pointed out that neither of the Special Investigative Reports made on Ochoa support the prosecution's claims that Ochoa was doing anything improper.

"Well, Your Honor, Mr. Ochoa suggested to the Patinos that they record any incriminating conversations they happened to hear."

"Would this have been wrong if the prosecution did that?"

"Oh no, Your Honor." They obviously had gone much further themselves — yet, as Schwartz left the stand, she still seemed unconvinced that the trial had been unfair.

When McMurdy called Steve Mitchell, the trial prosecutor, now moved on to a lucrative private practice, Mitchell "recalled" even less than Schwartz had. Ultimately, the prosecution rested with this strategy: if we don't admit to having done anything wrong, you can't prove we did, and even if Ochoa was incompetent, the only evidence presented in this case still shows Willoughby was guilty. Bizarre as it seems, this point of view prevailed to a certain extent in the Knapp murder trial, where the sitting judge had ruled that, despite clear evidence the prosecution repeatedly had violated Knapp's rights by suppressing evidence, the charges against Knapp could not be dismissed because it was impossible to prove their motive was to secure a false conviction.

Finally, Judge Howe "continued" Willoughby's hearing -- that is, postponed the rest of it -- to allow both sides to gather additional evidence. In October 1998, Dan was sent back to death row for another year.

On my way back to my office the day this hearing was continued, I recalled how much better Mitchell's memory had been on local radio talk shows. "It was a terrific experience for me. I became personally involved in the case. It was a great life experience for me," Mitchell said on a radio show called "Strauss' Place" in November of '93, at the height of enjoying his temporary celebrity for prosecuting Willoughby. Mitchell won the National Trial Award for 1993-94 and the Prosecutor of the Year Award from the AG's Office for 1991-92 for, according to Strauss, "successfully prosecuting one of the most high profile, without question one of the most bizarre, one of the most fascinating and intriguing and complex murder cases I've ever seen in the state of Arizona — or anywhere."

Mitchell told Strauss the AG's Office was notified of the murder by the homicide division of the Gilbert Police Department. "So we didn't go after Dan Willoughby," Mitchell insisted. "We went after whoever was responsible for the murder of Trish Willoughby." Strauss did not ask him how this could be true when the Gilbert police never took jurisdiction over this case and it was Kay Lines who first contacted them. He didn't ask him who else was investigated. The only other "lead" in the case was a report of three men in a black pickup seen leaving the area around the time of the murder; at trial, Mitchell pointedly told the jury there never had been any other suspects.

Mitchell specifically denied that the Huishes motivated this investigation — and no sooner had he said so than Strauss received an on-the-air phone call from Thera Huish applauding Mitchell's work. Strauss invited her to the radio party, treating his listeners to ten minutes of high-fiving and back-patting. Mitchell praised the Huishes as a "strong family," "survivors," and "religious people" who came out of this surprisingly well. Thera's son Nick and husband Sterling also called in on other lines to express mutual support for Mitchell.

Thera informed the audience that she had watched the mental abuse Dan put Trish through for a year before the murder. "I knew from the very first time I heard Dan Willoughby's voice in Mexico that he had murdered our daughter." According to Thera, Dan had told Trish that, if she ever left him, he would "take her down and have her children."

"Will Dan Willoughby be put to death?" Strauss asked the Huishes.

"I certainly hope so," they responded, almost in unison.

Well, if the Huishes didn't initiate the investigation of Dan Willoughby, who did, Mr. Mitchell?

"Things were said to us. Neighbors had mentioned family difficulties. Neighbors had mentioned marital infidelities — by Dan Willoughby. They had talked about large amounts of insurance proceeds that were available. So that interested us. The fact that an Arizona citizen was killed in Mexico interested us." Curiously, not a single one of these "neighbors" testified to any of these things at trial. There is no evidence to suggest that any neighbor knew anything whatsoever about insurance money. The prosecution apparently found only one individual outside the Huish clan who would testify that Trish had ever mentioned being "abused" by Dan, and outsiders who were closer to the family, such as Jamie Tepp and Jodie Critchfield, reported that nothing like that ever had occurred.

According to Mitchell, two days after Dan took Yesenia to Rocky Point to see the "death house," they had their "engagement" photos taken. (It is easy to imagine Yesenia characterizing the outing like this in her trial testimony, just as she had characterized her ring as an engagement ring, which it could not have been.) Mitchell explained they did the murder for both money and as a romantic game. From her pickup truck, Yesenia was to watch Dan put the kids in his van, go back into house to murder his wife; then, after he left, she was to go in and clean up. (Mitchell ignored the details of Marsha having changed her plan to stay behind at the last minute, and the fact that Trish herself didn't decide to stay home until after Dan and Yesenia already had met that morning.) The murder weapon was "savage, cruel, an archaic mace" — an eight-pound metal ball on heavy twine. (Yesenia, who has provided the only description of a murder weapon, actually called it "a BB on a string.") Mitchell himself had to admit he'd never seen it; "it wasn't recovered because Rocky Point has such a small, unsophisticated police force." Mitchell claimed that Yesenia says she threw it into a dumpster next to the house, which certainly would have required police incompetence to overlook. Of course, Dan himself never had an opportunity to dispose of anything, so his diabolical cleverness couldn't have been at play here. "Dan Willoughby struck her at least nine times," Mitchell insists. "Dr. Karnitschnig told the jury that in twenty years as medical examiner he'd never seen a skull so badly crushed, even by a car. But sending the kids back into the house knowing what they'd find is even worse." There was no mention at trial of the fact that the AG's Office had filed complaints against this very medical examiner for incompetence on several prior occasions; Kay Lines had done so personally. In this particular investigation, Karnitschnig failed even to record any of the stab wounds which had been so obvious to the Mexican medical examiner who had declared those wounds, indisputably made by Yesenia, the cause of death.

Dan Willoughby must be some kind of incredible monster, Strauss logically concluded.

"In person," Mitchell said, "Willoughby seems like a completely normal guy who fools everybody. He told his coworkers, `If you can surround yourself with people you can manipulate, you can control the world.' Combined with his evil mind, that made him a tremendously dangerous person." Mitchell is inaccurate, as far as I see from the trial transcript: only one coworker could be found to testify against Dan, a disgruntled former employee who had been fired for a variety of offenses. Furthermore, Mitchell fails to mention that Willoughby offered to submit to a lie detector test, the results of which could be used in court if both sides so agreed before it was administered. Mitchell had refused to agree.

"Who was the bigger monster here?" asked Strauss, after listening to Mitchell's account of the horrible murder.

"In my mind, unquestionably Dan Willoughby. Yesenia was a willing accomplice. She was an amoral accomplice. She was a decadent human being. And I think Dan Willoughby liked all of those qualities.... He, of course didn't know at the time he was dealing with a transsexual. She was as interesting a character as you can ever meet," he concluded, almost wistfully, past tense being appropriate for someone serving a 35-year sentence for first degree murder in Mexico.

I think of the last time I saw Dan, hands and ankles chained, limping out of Judge Howe's courtroom as his hearing for a new trial was continued once again. One ankle was ace bandaged, contributing to Nick Huish's mockery of "the Danny Shuffle." His shoulders looked demuscled, almost skeletal. The conservatively cut hair he sported when he was first arrested is tied into a long, greasy gray pony-tail, hanging half-way down the back of his gray and white striped prison garb. The pink sleeves were a mockery of color. His face was flaccid and drawn, almost waxen, his cheekbones and jaw sunken. He had never mentioned losing a cap and having his lower bridge broken, both of which the State refused to repair.

And yet, as I watched him, it was clear he had absolutely no intention of accepting death.

Siegel

Chapter 18: Deep Blue

What we have always wanted is an **unchangeable***, and we have found that only a compass point, a thought, an individual ideal, does not change.*

— John Steinbeck, **The Log from the** SEA OF CORTEZ.

Yesenia's confession does not guarantee Dan's acquittal, or even a new trial. Courts are skeptical of situations involving recanted testimony. Because the confessor is admitting to having lied once, what credibility should be given to the second version? And how does one determine which of the two versions of a story told by a liar, if either, really is the true one?

Motivation is one answer. Yesenia was promised great things by the prosecution for her testimony, or at least she believed she was. She believed she would go free in the United States after receiving only a light sentence in Mexico, based on the intervention of grateful American prosecutors with the Mexican judicial system. Well, Steve Mitchell apparently kept his promise to recommend leniency in Mexico and did not prosecute her at all in Arizona, but the Mexican court gave her the maximum sentence of 35 years anyway. As a juror, will you believe her anger at this outcome was a sufficient reason for her to disavow her prior, truthful testimony? Or will you believe Yesenia, when she says that she is motivated by guilt at having condemned an innocent man? Her insistence on Willoughby's innocence gains some weight when you consider that her recantation carries a price: she may be tried for both murder and perjury in the United States because she has violated her plea bargain.

Strikingly, her motive to commit the murder is consistent with her motive to confess to it now.

This is what Yesenia says:

I loved Dan and I didn't want to share him with anyone. He told me he wasn't having sex with his wife anymore, but then he told me he was taking his wife and kids down to Rocky Point and I got jealous. I was down there with him a little before that and he showed me this house that a friend of his owned on the beach where he was thinking of taking them. We tried to get in, but the door was locked. He said he would take me there too, after his family, but I got jealous.

I told Tony he had to take me to Rocky Point the day before the murder because I needed to collect some money for Dan Willoughby that was owed him by somebody. I paid him $500 to drive. The night before we left, I stole the mace from the El Capri Dance Club, and I hid it in my purse so Tony never saw it. We went to Manny's and Dan showed up, and boy was he surprised to see me. "What are you doing here?" he says, and I tell him I cannot be without him. "What if my wife sees us?" he says, and I told him that I didn't care. So he takes us to another restaurant — Tony's there too, but he's off in his own little world, he has no clue what's going on. So Dan takes us to another restaurant for a beer and to calm me down, and after I tell him, OK, I'm going back home. Dan says, OK, he's taking his family sight-seeing.

When he leaves, I go into the bathroom with my cocaine and heroin and a spoon and a syringe. I mix up the coke and shoot it into my left arm, like this, and then I do the same thing with the heroin. Then I throw the syringe in the garbage. I brought this stuff with me because I knew I was going to kill Trish.

Then I dropped Tony off in the plaza across from the police station and told him I was going to get the money. I parked about a block away from the house. The kids were playing outside. I didn't like something about Marsha, but I liked the two little ones. I watched them for about an hour, and then Dan came out and got into the van. Then Dan got out of the van and went back to the front door and did something, then came back to the van and they left.

I moved the truck closer ιͻ the house and parked behind it in an empty lot and walked up to the back door. It was latched on the inside, but I got a nail and got it unlatched. Then I went in quietly, like a robber, into the bedroom where Trish was laying. She was wearing a white blouse and jeans and had a paperback book on her face with the word "Matol" on the cover. Trish looked up and saw me, but before she could say anything I hit her with the mace.

I swung it over my head, like this, and I hit her six times. The first time knocked her out. She didn't make any sounds.

But she was still breathing. So I went into the kitchen to look for knives. No, I didn't have any gloves on. I was looking for some sharper knives, but all I got was butter knives, some smaller knives. There was a lot of blood. It didn't bother me then, but the next day.... I don't want to talk about it anymore.

I never talked to Dan about it, before or after, and he never asked me. I don't care about him any more, except that he is an innocent man I have done something to. He wrote to me sometimes, but he never sent me any money or anything.

When the TV news people were here from Telemundo, I made up a card with a drawing of myself behind bars crying for him and said I loved him. He never writes to me any more. I don't love him.

In horror movies, monsters always are shaken from centuries of sleep by cataclysmic events: an earthquake that breaks open the long-sealed cave, an eruption that melts the glacier. At the very least, someone dusts off a prophetic curse, deaf to the orchestra's falling chord. But it is not great events that move men. These pass over us. A woman in love with another's husband, a man who loves his wife but feels he's unappreciated and panics that life is passing him by, a mother distraught at the loss of her daughter and righteously angry at the man who has mistreated her, an adversarial justice system thrown out of balance by the best intentions, these all can kill people.

Monday morning are the closing arguments for Dan Willoughby's hearing for a new trial. For over a year now, the Attorney General's Office and Dan's new attorneys have argued about whether David Ochoa's legal representation of Willoughby was so ineffective that he deserves another trial before a jury. The standard of proof for Dan is very high. It is not good enough to prove his defense might have been better than it was, or that Ochoa made some obvious mistakes. Dan must show that Ochoa was so completely incompetent that the jury probably reached their guilty verdict because of that incompetence.

The evidence that Dan Willoughby deserves a new trial for the murder of his wife seems overwhelming to me, but such criminal appeals are rarely granted. If his is not, he will almost certainly be executed. All Dan can do is go to the hearing, listen to the attorneys for both sides sum up, and wait for Judge Howe's ruling.

The Saturday before final arguments on Dan's Motion for a New Trial, we sit in the beige plastic chairs at the Madison Street jail in Phoenix. The walls are beige, the folding table a familiar fake wood plastic. It will be a while before I buy anything brownish. It's maybe five feet by eight feet, almost twice the size of his cell in Supermax (Special Management Unit II) back in Florence, Dan tells me. (J. E. Relly in *Tucson Weekly* describes these cells as the institutional version of a straitjacket.) Dan's out of that windowless cell for exactly three hours a week, when he's allowed out into an equally windowless room about twice this size for "recreation." The black and white horizontal striped jumpsuit does nothing for his figure, but he's stylin' in Sheriff Arpaio's pink long johns, pink socks, orange tennies, and stainless-steel ankle bracelets. We've been talking for a couple of hours, and I have to go back to my family, on the other side of the airlock from this place.

Dan is a very bright, upper-middle class sixty-year-old guy, and, absolutely incredible to me, he seems to have kept both his sanity and sense of humor after eight years of this. He's been telling me anecdotes from death row that might get him killed if I were to repeat them here, although some appear merely comic and inconsequential to me while others concern multiple murderers complaining about being convicted of the wrong crime. But as I'm about to go, he says, "I know you guys," meaning lawyers, "don't like to hear this stuff, but I've got to tell you."

He's right. I know what's coming, and I don't want to hear it, except maybe out of a morbid curiosity. He's going to try to convince me he didn't murder his wife by telling me about The Big Moment. And because he is a very bright guy, and a salesman to boot, I'm never going to accept what he says, no matter how convincing. Let somebody else look into his eyes and tell you what he sees. Let Judge Howe figure out if there's anyone with wings in his courtroom. I'll always be an agnostic.

I think Dan knows that, but he goes on anyway. "Thinnes thinks I might get offered a deal where they'll let me plead to time served. I win on Monday, I can walk without a retrial if I help them save face by saying I killed my wife."

"Maybe they'd give you a *nolo contendere*," I said, "like Spiro Agnew. After you got out, you could still say you never admitted the charge, you just agreed not to contest it."

"I'm still pleading to something. I can't do that, because, well....

"After Trish died, the Mexican authorities had me come down to their morgue to identify her. It's a tiny little room, not much bigger than this, mostly a huge ice chest about four feet high. On top are these two big drawers, like file cabinet drawers, and they pull out one of them, only it sticks, like there's something caught in there, and I hear this ripping sound. When I open my eyes, it's not Trish. It's some naked guy. Wrong drawer. They open up the other one, and there she is. Her head is shaved on top and in the front, where all the uh, you know, were. You know what I mean? And I just looked at her, and I thought, I'm going to get the sonofabitch that did this. Well...."

He pauses. We're waiting for the guards to take him back down now, and I don't know what conjunction to put here for him, "but" or "and." "I've been reading a lot of law in my spare time. They don't turn the lights on in our pod until about three in the afternoon, but you can read by this little night-light thing. Maybe you know this, but you can be criminally ignorant: reckless indifference, wanton indifference, I think they call it. If I'd ever imagined Yesenia was a threat to Trish, or to any of the kids, there's no way I would have let her anywhere near them. Even that morning, when I saw her at Manny's, I would have done something. But it just never occurred to me. Now, I don't know how I couldn't have seen it. I just didn't. And I'm going to live with that for the rest of my life. It was my fault. I don't mean the adultery. I mean, it was my fault, because I was so incredibly blind...."

Rex has managed to hook me up with an actual phone call to the United States. Carole wants to know where I am, how I am. The phone connection is lousey, and it is hard to pretend to be off-hand when you have to scream into the mouthpiece.

"I'm right where you left me," I say.

"I was hoping you'd grown up since then," she retorts.

"In the last thirty years, or since last week?"

"What are you doing?"

"Frenchy and I are training for the Old Boys Poker Run. We go to five different bars and get a drink and a card at each one. The guy with the best hand at the end of the night wins."

"And you're trying to memorize the deck?"

"Something like that."

She sighs. "Why don't you come home so we can scream at each other in person?"

"OK," I say. I wish I could tell her that I managed to get Rex beaten up by the Federales who thought he was the gringo who fought with Stephano Brown. I wish I could tell her my latest insights about how human lives intersect, about how much pain we cause and how much time we waste by imagining we're the center of every little universe in the bigger one. Because Yesenia imagined she was more important to Dan than she was, she killed an innocent woman and destroyed several other lives. Because I imagined I was more than a prop in Sophie's relationship with Stephano, I nearly ruined the relationship that was at the center of my own universe. But I will not risk it, because insights do not excuse actions.

I hope, after all this, you do not think I am trivializing the Willoughby tragedy by comparing it to my own petty bumblings. My intention is exactly the opposite. Trish remains dead, Dan's life ruined, their children orphaned under terrible circumstances. There is no insight I can have, nothing I can tell you that will help that.

The wind rises as I am packing to leave Rocky Point, and I imagine it igniting the flight of a million airborne seeds from the palm trees in our back yard in Phoenix, each explosive seed with the potential to destroy my mental daguerreotype of the yard with new life. The wind rises to keep me here or blow me off the face of these Mexican shores, which I cannot tell. I am, after all of this, just a tourist. What I have learned here is that nothing very dramatic happens to most of us, and that, when it does, we manage to get over it.

But suddenly I hear something so startling and eerie that everything else around me simply melts away as I am sucked into the pure reel of the sound, the brass voice of a god.

Bev and Don are already on the veranda when I get there, staring down the beach. They are holding hands as if they were children. "Sonofabitch," Don mutters. "It works." The Breath of God rolls over all of us, something come from across the sky.

I do not pretend to know what it means.

Postscript

I began this book in 1995 by talking to Grave Danger and taking the trip to Rocky Point that is described in the first few chapters of this book. Since then, I have been back many times, and later autobiographical events are compressed from those various other visits. The last scene in the book is, sadly, merely imagined, because Don Glasenapp died of pancreatic cancer shortly after I came to know him.

Yet my intention in ending with this scene of the improbable and whimsical Breath of God ringing over the bay seems to me born out by events. Don looked remarkably healthy in 1995, and was dead within a matter of months. Dan Willoughby, languishing on death row, was losing appeal after appeal, desperately clinging to the wet porcelain funnel of his reality. Then, in November of 1999, two days after the first edition of this book appeared on the internet, his conviction for murdering his wife was overturned. A few days ago, he was taken off death row and returned to the county jail, to await word if he will be retried, offered a plea bargain for time served, or simply released, a free, but very, very different man.

Logically, one would expect the state to retry Dan only if they felt they had a reasonable case. This could be true despite Judge Howe's recent finding that, had Dan had an effective attorney, it is reasonably probable he might not have been convicted. In other words, Dan has not been found innocent; his conviction has been voided because his trial wasn't fair. Back in 1984, in a case called *Strickland v. Washington*, the United States Supreme Court ruled that a defendant's consitutional right to a fair trial was violated if his lawyer made such severe mistakes that it was reasonably probable that, but for these errors, the defendant would not have been convicted. In the Willoughby hearing on ineffective assistance of counsel, the state really only argued one prong of a two-part test. Even the state's aggressive appellate attorney, Paul McMurdie, had difficulty claiming with a straight face that Ochoa's performance had been adequate, but he argued vigorously that the results of the trial would have been the same anyway.

Willoughby's appellate attorney, Gil Levy, argued not only that Ochoa's representation had been ineffective, but that Ochoa had acted improperly by giving priority to his own fears of being prosecuted for witness tampering if he vigorously defended Dan, and that the State was guilty of misconduct in creating that conflict of interest in the first place by attacking Ochoa personally. Judge Howe never had to decide the second and third issues. Howe found that Ochoa's defense at trial was unreasonably deficient under the circumstances of the case, and that it was reasonable to assume that that deficiency had led to Willoughby's conviction and death sentence. On November 17, 1999, Judge Howe vacated the 1992 judgment and sentence and ordered a retrial.

Judge Howe declared that Ochoa "set the stage" for his ineffective assistance in his opening statement, when "he presented a pervasive, repetitive, ringing denunciation of his client as a sinner, liar, blackmailer, conniver, betrayer and cheat. Then he played directly into the state's case by offering a theory which he made up, nearly from whole cloth, that, as the state alleged, his client and [Yesenia] Patino did conspire against the decedent; that, yes, they did do so for money; that, yes, they lured the decedent to Rocky Point, Mexico, in the guise of a family vacation; that, yes, defendant was to get his family away from decedent, leaving the decedent alone in the rented house; that, yes, defendant did unlock the rented house's back door to allow in Patino; and, yes, Patino came into the house to get money from the decedent. Here, [defense] counsel said, the conspiracy was to get the money by blackmail, not murder: that Patino would threaten to take defendant away from the decedent unless the decedent paid her money. It was just, said defense counsel, that the plan went awry."

Judge Howe never commented on how stupid Ochoa's scenario was. (Why take someone to a secluded spot in Mexico, away from her bank account, to blackmail her? Why not call her at her home in Phoenix?) Rather, he observed, "Thus, defense counsel had pleaded his client guilty to felony-murder-for-money, death being the punishment, disagreeing only in the motive for the murder."

Next Judge Howe focused on the state's allegation that Willoughby had murdered his wife for the insurance money, the "aggravating circumstance" compelling the death sentence he received. Howe's ruling points out that there was no admissible evidence Dan even knew the insurance policies existed and a good deal of admissible evidence, never presented by Ochoa, that he didn't know about the policies. Ochoa utterly failed to defend his client, allowing Thera Huish to testify that she "assumed" Willoughby knew about the policies even though she had no foundation for that belief other than her conviction Dan was a murderer. Then Ochoa failed to call either of the insurance agents who could have testified that they had been instructed not to tell Dan about the existence of the policies, both before and after the murder, and that Dan apparently had no knowledge of the policies until another agent tracked them through his agency while Dan was trying to settle his wife's estate several months later.

Third, Judge Howe zeroed in on Ochoa's failure to impeach Yesenia's testimony with her tape-recorded confession that she had committed the murder alone and without Dan's knowledge, and that she was going to lie on the stand to protect her brother Tony from retaliatory charges threatened by the prosecution. Without Yesenia's testimony, the state had, at most, circumstantial evidence tying Willoughby to the murder.

Finally, Judge Howe listed a series of other examples of Ochoa's "below-standard trial conduct." These included his failure to rebut the state's claim that there was no evidence of a dark pickup truck at the scene of the crime, which Dan claimed he'd been told by the Mexican police and of which there was, in fact, a report. (Willoughby was convicted of obstructing an investigation because of this claim.) Howe decried Ochoa's introduction of the inflamatory and horrifying "exemplar" murder weapons, which the jury never would have been allowed to see if the state had tried to introduce them. Howe noted that several other arguments, such as that a competent counsel could have limited the "Mafia" comments, did not rise to the level necessary to require a new trial, but that, based "[o]n the totality of the evidence," Willoughby's guilty verdict had to be overturned.

As a lawyer who has been over much (but not all) of the evidence, I don't think the state has a very strong case against Dan. Without Yesenia's confession, there is only circumstantial evidence and speculation tying him to the murder. Of course, it is perfectly possible for a man to be convicted purely on circumstantial evidence, if the circumstantial evidence is convincing. If you see snow falling on the court house steps in Phoenix, you have direct evidence that it has snowed. If you exit the courtroom and find the snow on the ground, you have circumstantial evidence it snowed. This is a common example of compelling circumstantial evidence from which a reasonable person might assume the fact that it has snowed. While it is remotely possible that a ski resort sponsoring a special event has dumped the snow there, a juror probably would conclude, beyond a reasonable doubt, that it had snowed. It would be the defendant's job to show that the ski resort's snow-laden trucks had been in the vicinity. In the Willoughby murder, there are a lot of trucks driving around the scene of the crime.

Still, the state may be too embarrassed simply to let Dan Willoughby go free. The Arizona Attorney General is an elected office, and public perception may be an important factor in the state's decision. Grant Woods, the Republican AG whom originally indicted Willoughby, is no longer in office, and so it might be a lesser embarrassment for the newly elected Democratic AG, Janet Napolitano, to announce that a mistake had been made and let Dan walk out of his jail cell. However, as the first elected woman AG in Arizona history, AG Napolitano would not want to appear soft on crime, and therefore might insist on a retrial. Alternatively, she might offer Willoughby a face-saving alternative, a plea bargain for "time served." In exchange for admitting that he conspired to murder his wife, Dan's death sentence would be reduced to the seven-plus years of prison time he already has served. While it would be expedient for Dan to accept such a deal, he has so far refused to consider it, since even a "nolo contendre" plea (not saying he did it but not contesting the state's claim that he did) is a tacit admission of a horrible deed he has denied vehemently since he was first accused.

As Alan Berlow reported in "The Wrong Man," Rolando Cruz was retried three times despite a credible confession from a convicted child murderer, exculpatory DNA evidence, and the complete lack of direct evidence against Cruz. Prosecutors continued with this case despite the resignation both of one of their own detectives, who was so convinced of the state's error that he offered to testify for the defense, and of an Assistant Attorney General, who protested the state was trying to execute an innocent man. Cruz's torment did not end until a judge literally ordered a directed verdict of innocence.

Judge Howe has set any new trial for July, 2000, so we may soon see. Stay tuned for Rocky.3.

In the end, whatever the legal outcome, I expect to remain something of an agnostic. As I have said all along, I am not enough of a sensitive or psychic to ever rest easily with my own perceptions of a man's protestations of innocence. Dan Willoughby has looked into my eyes and told me he never wished any harm to come to his wife. I do not disbelieve him, but I doubt my own ability to judge such avowals. At the same time, I have watched the Huish family through several court appearances providing a jeering section to Dan's protestations of innocence, and I am reminded, sadly, of Thera Huish's original comment on the day Dan Willoughby first was indicted: "All of the things I felt from the very beginning are now reality." An indictment did not prove Dan was really a murderer any more than Judge Howe's overturning a verdict proves Dan is incontrovertibly innocent. Thera would think me insane for suggesting that this latest turn of events means that "reality" is that Dan is innocent. Over the last eight years, the Huish family has directed its members' grief over the horrible and senseless death of a beloved daughter and sister at Dan Willoughby. To them, Judge Howe's latest ruling is a slap in the face, an insult to their feelings, not evidence that they may have misdirected their grief and anger. They are still confirmed in their belief that "reality" is that Dan is a murderer, even though it is no longer the officially sanctioned reality. There will be no resolution, no healing for them here.

When God's Breath blows through the world of man, it confirms not what we know of reality, but how distant and present, tangible and yet inscrutable, reality may be.

T-Shirt has lost some weight and is looking good. Eat your heart out, Hemingway.

My Imaginary Mistress remains completely imaginary, as does her husband, the non-existent Stevie.

The End

Siegel

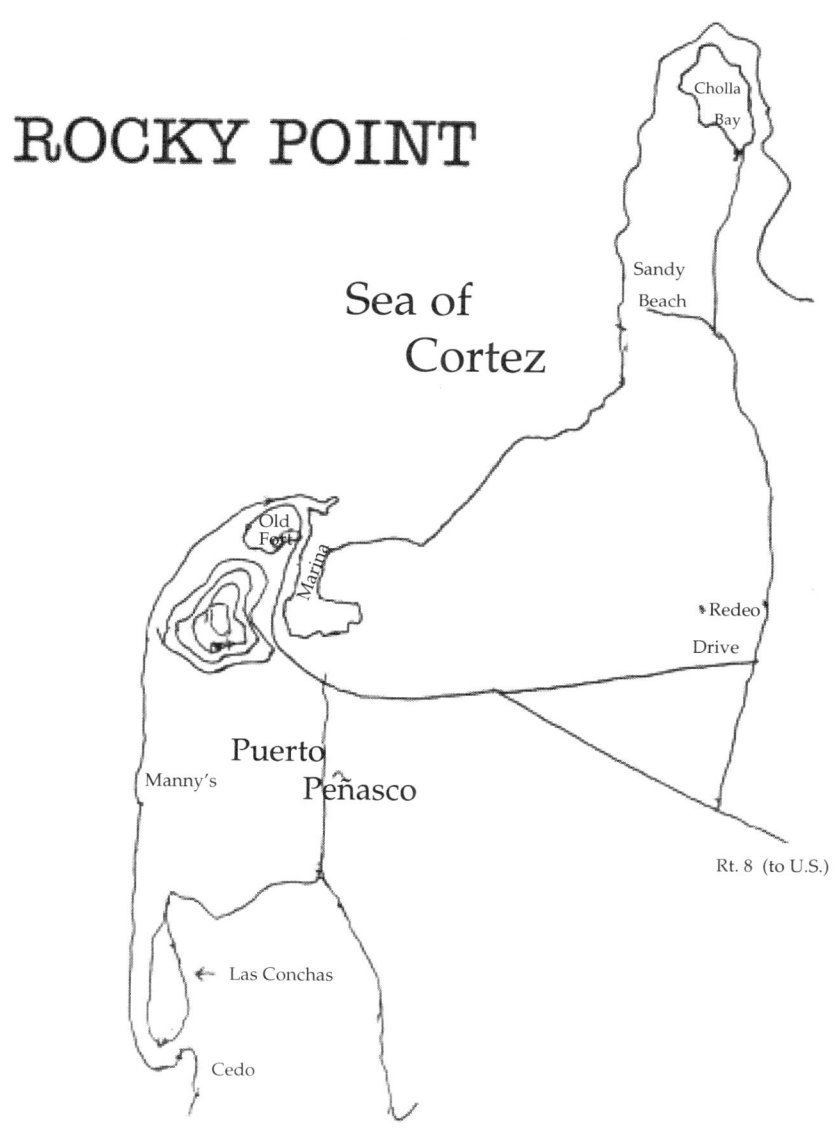

ROCKY POINT

Sea of
Cortez

Cholla
Bay

Sandy
Beach

Old
Fort

Marina

Redeo
Drive

Puerto
Peñasco

Manny's

Rt. 8 (to U.S.)

← Las Conchas

Cedo